YORK NOTES

# A Man for All Seasons

### Robert Bolt

Notes by Bernard Haughey

 Longman

 York Press

Bernard Haughey is hereby identified as author of this work in accordance with Section 77 of the Copyright, Designs and Patents Act 1988

YORK PRESS
322 Old Brompton Road, London SW5 9JH

PEARSON EDUCATION LIMITED
Edinburgh Gate, Harlow,
Essex CM20 2JE, United Kingdom
Associated companies, branches and representatives throughout the world

First published 1999

ISBN 0-582-38228-9

Designed by Vicki Pacey
Illustrations by Chris Price
Phototypeset by Gem Graphics, Trenance, Mawgan Porth, Cornwall
Colour reproduction and film output by Spectrum Colour
Produced by Addison Wesley Longman China Limited, Hong Kong

# CONTENTS

# PREFACE

York Notes are designed to give you a broader perspective on works of literature studied at GCSE and equivalent levels. We have carried out extensive research into the needs of the modern literature student prior to publishing this new edition. Our research showed that no existing series fully met students' requirements. Rather than present a single authoritative approach, we have provided alternative viewpoints, empowering students to reach their own interpretations of the text. York Notes provide a close examination of the work and include biographical and historical background, summaries, glossaries, analyses of characters, themes, structure and language, cultural connections and literary terms.

If you look at the Contents page you will see the structure for the series. However, there's no need to read from the beginning to the end as you would with a novel, play, poem or short story. Use the Notes in the way that suits you. Our aim is to help you with your understanding of the work, not to dictate how you should learn.

York Notes are written by English teachers and examiners, with an expert knowledge of the subject. They show you how to succeed in coursework and examination assignments, guiding you through the text and offering practical advice. Questions and comments will extend, test and reinforce your knowledge. Attractive colour design and illustrations improve clarity and understanding, making these Notes easy to use and handy for quick reference.

York Notes are ideal for:
- Essay writing
- Exam preparation
- Class discussion

The author of these Notes is Bernard Haughey, BA, a former head of English who has taught in a variety of technical colleges, grammar and comprehensive schools. He is an examiner for a major GCSE examinations board. He is the author of the York Note on *David Copperfield* by Charles Dickens.

The text used in these Notes is the edition with notes by E.R. Wood in the Heinemann 'Hereford Plays' series.

*Health Warning:* **This study guide will enhance your understanding, but should not replace the reading of the original text and/or study in class.**

# PART ONE

# INTRODUCTION

## HOW TO STUDY A PLAY

You have bought this book because you wanted to study a play on your own. This may supplement classwork.

* Drama is a special 'kind' of writing (the technical term is 'genre') because it needs a performance in the theatre to arrive at a full interpretation of its meaning. When reading a play you have to imagine how it should be performed; the words alone will not be sufficient. Think of gestures and movements.

* Drama is always about conflict of some sort (it may be below the surface). Identify the conflicts in the play and you will be close to identifying the large ideas or themes which bind all the parts together.

* Make careful notes on themes, characters, plot and any sub-plots of the play.

* Playwrights find non-realistic ways of allowing an audience to see into the minds and motives of their characters. The 'soliloquy', in which a character speaks directly to the audience, is one such device. Does the play you are studying have any such passages?

* Which characters do you like or dislike in the play? Why? Do your sympathies change as you see more of these characters?

* Think of the playwright writing the play. Why were these particular arrangements of events, these particular sets of characters and these particular speeches chosen?

Studying on your own requires self-discipline and a carefully thought-out work plan in order to be effective. Good luck.

# Robert Bolt's Background

*His family*    Robert Bolt was born in 1924 to Nonconformist parents in Sale near Manchester. His father owned a shop which sold furniture (some antique), china and glassware, and his mother taught in a primary school.

*His education*    Though Bolt attended the prestigious Manchester Grammar School, he was a disruptive pupil and academically unsuccessful. On leaving school at sixteen, he drifted aimlessly into insurance, but hated the work and was bad at it.

To gain university entrance, Bolt studied three subjects at A-level and, after only five weeks' work, achieved his goal. He read history at Manchester University and joined the Communist Party while he was there.

*War service*    In 1943, after completing a year of his course, he was conscripted for war service and joined the RAF. He suffered from air sickness, so failed his aircrew training and was redrafted into the army, with which he served in the Gold Coast (now Ghana). Even while an officer in His Majesty's forces, he remained a member of the Communist Party.

*Teacher and aspiring playwright*    Bolt left the army in 1946 with the rank of lieutenant and resumed his degree course at Manchester University. He hated the industrial environment of Manchester and on gaining his degree left the city, never to return. He took a teaching diploma at Exeter University and began his career as a teacher at a village school in Devon. In 1950 he wrote the school's nativity play and came to realise that he wanted to take up a new career as a playwright.

*His first success*    From 1952 to 1958 he taught at Millfield School in Somerset. During this period he produced radio plays for both children and adults, which the BBC broadcast. One of these was an early version of *A Man for All Seasons*. His first success in the theatre was with the *Flowering Cherry* produced in London in 1957. It won the *Evening Standard* award for the most promising play. The play is a domestic drama about a frustrated insurance salesman and has, therefore, some relevance to his own life.

*A Man for All Seasons*

In 1960, the year the stage version of *A Man for All Seasons* opened in London, it won the New York Drama Critics' Circle Award.

*Drama and the playwright's life*

*The Tiger and the Horse* (1961) also dealt with the conflict between the conscience of the individual and the demands of authority. Again this reflected Bolt's own life, because, as a member of the Campaign for Nuclear Disarmament's (CND's) Committee of a Hundred, he was involved in protests against the government's nuclear arms policy. He was arrested after a CND 'Ban the Bomb' march and imprisoned for refusing to be bound over to keep the peace. Since, at that time, he was writing the screenplay for the film, *Lawrence of Arabia*, and his imprisonment was costing the film studio money and jobs, he was persuaded to accept the terms for his release, but felt he had become a traitor to his true self.

*The influence of Brecht*

The author claimed that his work was influenced by Brecht, whose aim was to stimulate a critical detachment of the audience rather than passive acceptance. Certainly, with the character of the Common Man, Bolt uses Brecht's technique of interrupting the action of the play with switches of role and **ironic** (see Literary Terms) comment by the narrator. The aims of Brecht and Bolt also coincide here in the attempt to encourage a rational view of history as something that is developed by human actions and not as a passive process.

*Work for the cinema*

Bolt's film scripts included those of *Doctor Zhivago, The Mission* (which won the *Palme d'Or* at Cannes in 1986), *A Man for All Seasons, Lady Caroline Lamb, Ryan's*

*Daughter* and *The Bounty*. It was while working on this last script that Bolt suffered a stroke which paralysed him and affected his speech.

Robert Bolt was married twice and had four children. He married Celia Ann Roberts in 1949 and, later, the actress Sarah Miles. He died in 1995.

# CONTEXT AND SETTING

*The struggle for power*

The Wars of the Roses (1455–85), the power struggle between the houses of York and Lancaster, had caused thirty years of bloodshed and decimated the aristocracy. The wars ended at the Battle of Bosworth in 1485, when the forces of the Lancastrian, Henry Tudor, defeated those of the Yorkist king, Richard III, who was killed. Henry Tudor took the crown as Henry VII.

The feuding factions of York and Lancaster were united by the marriage of Henry VII to Elizabeth of York.

*Henry VIII's need for a male heir*

The future Henry VIII, the son of Henry VII and Elizabeth of York, was born in 1491 and the recent civil war must have coloured his childhood. Certainly, it was seen as the monarch's duty to do all in his power to ensure such slaughter would not recur. It was the opinion of the time that a strong ruler meant a male ruler. Hence Henry's obsession with having a legitimate male heir.

*Was the marriage valid?*

Henry VIII was crowned in 1509, at the age of eighteen, and married Catherine of Aragon, the aunt of Charles V of Spain, the same year. When only 14, Henry had objected to the proposed marriage because Catherine was the widow of his elder brother Arthur, and therefore, according to the Bible, Henry's marriage to Catherine would be incestuous (Leviticus 18:16). It

was necessary to get the pope's permission before the
marriage could take place.

*The pope
a prisoner*

Although Henry and Catherine had a daughter, the
future queen Mary I, Catherine failed to produce a son
and male heir to the throne. Henry came to regard this
as God's punishment for breaking his law. Cardinal
Wolsey, Henry's chancellor, was given the unenviable
task of persuading the pope to grant Henry a divorce.
Unfortunately for Henry's hopes, Charles V of Spain
had sacked Rome in 1527 and the pope was his
prisoner, in all but name, at the castle of San Angelo.
The pope delayed his verdict on Henry's divorce, as
much for political as moral reasons, so Henry decided
to take matters into his own hands. Wolsey, having
failed to give the king the divorce he wanted, was
accused of high treason, but died on his way to trial.

*Nationalism,
the divorce
and church
reform*

Reformation of the church was a topic raging
throughout Europe with Martin Luther as its driving
force. Rising nationalism meant that foreign
interference in English affairs was greatly resented. As a
result, the church and the pope faced increasing
criticism in England. The conditions were right for
Henry to break with Rome. Thomas More, who had
succeeded Wolsey as Henry's chancellor, was opposed
to any usurping of the pope's legitimate powers.

Thomas Cromwell became the king's servant after
Wolsey fell. His duty was to ensure that Henry's wishes
were put into practice. Cranmer was appointed
Archbishop of Canterbury and presided over Henry's
divorce, declaring that Henry's marriage to Catherine
had never been valid; therefore, his marriage to Anne
Boleyn was legitimate.

*The oath to
the Act of
Succession*

In 1534, it became compulsory for everyone to take the
oath to the Act of Succession. The wording of the oath
was such that whoever took it condemned Henry's first

marriage and accepted the legality of the second, making Anne's children heirs to the throne.

Thomas More and John Fisher, Bishop of Rochester, refused to take the oath and were imprisoned in the Tower of London. Later in the year a law was passed making it a treasonable offence to refuse to take the oath. Fisher and More were executed. Henry's authority as head of the church was now virtually unchallenged.

*England in Henry VIII's reign*

At the end of the fifteenth century England was a thinly populated country. Most people earned their living from agriculture or fishing and the only exports were sheep and wool. However, there was a rapid expansion of the cloth industry early in Henry's reign. By the king's death in 1547 exports of cloth had risen from 80,000 to 120,000 pieces of cloth in barely 30 years. The prosperity of the country also increased.

Although Henry VIII had inherited a sound treasury and an efficient administration from his father, he still became bankrupt. To refill his coffers he ordered the dissolution (closure) of the monasteries, selling most of the monastic lands to his courtiers. Henry spent a great deal of his newly gained wealth on the navy. He built dockyards at Woolwich and Deptford and developed a naval base at Portsmouth.

*Literature in sixteenth-century England.*

Much of the literature of the time was written in Latin and a great deal of what was written in English was translated from Latin. Thomas Wyatt and the Earl of Surrey were responsible for introducing the **Petrarchan sonnet** (see Literary Terms) into English from the Italian. Surrey also introduced **blank verse** (see Literary Terms). Both poets were published in *Tottel's Miscellany* (1559).

Erasmus, the great Dutch intellectual and friend of Thomas More, had his satire, *In Praise of Folly*, published in 1511. In it he condemns clerical abuses and praises Christian simplicity.

The **morality play**, *Everyman*, is from this period. It is written in **stanzas** and **rhyming couplets** (see Literary Terms) and traces the progress of its hero from complacency to despair and final resignation.

Thomas More's most famous English work is *Utopia*, published in Latin in 1516 and later in English and many other languages. It is a criticism of contemporary society and describes an island where the happy inhabitants hold property in common.

Henry VIII's tutor, John Skelton, was writing poems and satires at this time and upset Wolsey by attacking him in '*Speak Parrot, Colin Clout*'.

The setting of *A Man for all Seasons* is along the Thames from Hampton Court to the Tower of London. All the action takes place in this area.

# PART TWO

# SUMMARIES

## GENERAL SUMMARY

*Act I*

The play is introduced by the Common Man, who represents that which is common to us all. Richard Rich, a friend of Thomas More, is unhappy because he cannot persuade More to employ him. More realises that Rich is too weak to resist the temptations of political life and advises him to become a teacher.

Cardinal Wolsey, Henry VIII's chancellor, summons More to him late at night. Before leaving his house, More brings Rich to the attention of the Duke of Norfolk, but without recommending him for employment and Rich departs with the gift of a goblet, which More had been given as a bribe.

*Wolsey aims to win More's support.*

Wolsey tries without success to win More's support for a papal annulment of Henry's marriage to Catherine of Aragon, aunt of Charles V of Spain. Cromwell, Wolsey's secretary, and Chapuys, the Spanish ambassador, both meet More as he leaves Wolsey. Chapuys issues threats of trouble from Spain if Catherine is divorced.

When More arrives home, Margaret, his daughter, and William Roper, Margaret's future husband, are waiting for him. Roper asks permission to marry Margaret, but More refuses, on religious grounds. Roper's attitude is aggressively anti-church. More evades his daughter's and his wife, Alice's, questions about the meeting with Wolsey.

*More becomes chancellor.*

The death of Wolsey is announced and More becomes chancellor. Cromwell is now employed by the king. His duty is to act as a spy and to get the king's wishes accomplished. He knows all about Richard Rich, but

Chapuys's knowledge of the armament of the *Great Harry* is more accurate than his; Chapuys also knows the king's itinerary. Cromwell and Chapuys argue about More's attitude to the king's 'great matter'.

*Henry visits More.*

More's household and his friend, the Duke of Norfolk, are in a panic because the king is due on a visit and More cannot be found. Although Henry is friendly towards More hoping to win his support in divorcing Catherine, he makes it very clear that he will allow no opposition, which he would regard as treason.

*Cromwell employs Rich.*

After Henry's departure, More's wife, Alice, shows her uncompromising opposition to her husband's stance. Rich begs More to employ him, again without success, whereupon Rich goes to see Cromwell, who is flushed with success at his recent promotion. Cromwell sounds out Rich to see whether he is a suitable tool for his purpose. Cromwell proclaims that expediency is his rule in life and promises Rich the position of Collector of Revenues for York.

*Act II*

Two years have elapsed and the Church of England has been established. More and Roper disagree as to its character. Chapuys accuses More of being party to Henry's action and wants him to spark off a revolution in the north. Norfolk announces that the bishops have succumbed to Henry's will and the church has separated from Rome. More interprets this surrender as the destruction of the Catholic Church in England, not its reformation, and resigns from his position as chancellor. More warns Norfolk of the possibility of a rebellion in the north.

*The bishops give in to Henry.*

*More's family lives in poverty.*

Alice cannot understand More's attitude and complains about the deterioration in their standard of living. Cromwell is determined that More will swear allegiance to the changed constitution and makes an unsuccessful effort to undermine his reputation by accusing him of accepting bribes.

Chapuys brings More a letter from the King of Spain, which More refuses to accept. Cromwell summons the former chancellor to answer charges, but is unable to trap him into treasonable statements.

*More is now in danger.*

Since it is now dangerous to be seen as a friend of Thomas More, he picks an artificial argument with his friend, Norfolk, to make it easier for the duke to break off their friendship.

*More imprisoned.*

An Act of Parliament has been passed making it compulsory for everyone to swear an oath of allegiance agreeing to the Act of Succession. More will not take the oath and is imprisoned. He steadfastly refuses to give a reason for his refusal.

Margaret, Alice and Roper are allowed to visit More in order to persuade him to relent. Though he fears for his family, he cannot betray his inner self and begs them to leave the country.

*More's trial is rigged.*

Thomas More is brought to trial on a charge of high treason. More and Cromwell debate the meaning of 'Silence gives consent'. Richard Rich gives false evidence, which More refutes. Because vital witnesses have been sent to other parts of the country, More cannot directly prove Rich's perjury and is condemned to death. After the verdict is given and judgement passed, More makes plain his opposition to Henry's marriage to Anne Boleyn and goes to his death 'merrily'.

# Detailed Summaries

## ACT I

### Part 1 (pages 1–25)

*Introduction to More's family and household.*

This play, concerned with great events and people of eminence, is introduced by the Common Man who uses several **transferred epithets** (see Literary Terms); 'common', as Bolt tells us in the Preface, in the sense of possessing 'that which is common to us all' and not in any derogatory sense. He, at once, becomes Thomas More's steward, setting the table and helping himself to the wine. On entering, More asks his steward about the quality of the wine knowing he has been sampling it.

*The lives of Rich and More run parallel to their views stated here.*

The first words we hear from Richard Rich, a friend of More's, are: 'But every man has his price' (p. 2). This is highly significant in the light of his future conduct. More considers Rich's further arguments on this topic to be childish. The Common Man despises Rich.

*Rich's ambition and avarice are seen early in the play.*

Rich admits uneasily that he has been in contact with Cromwell, who has hinted to him that that he could help him. More's comment upon Cromwell is guarded, to say the least. More knows Rich's weakness and advises him against going into politics, urging him instead to go back to Cambridge to sharpen up his mind. Rich would rather work for More, but he suggests only that Rich ought to take up the teaching post offered by the Dean of St Paul's, an offer scorned by Rich. More knows that Rich will be unable to resist the temptations of political office and gives him an Italian silver goblet he has received as a bribe, knowing perfectly well that Rich will sell it. Again he advises Rich to become a teacher, confiding to him that he (More) took office only under orders, a statement that Rich regards with some scepticism.

The Duke of Norfolk enters and immediately begins to argue with Alice, More's wife, about the ability of his

*Cromwell is a*
*cause of unease*
*from the start.*

falcon. In the course of a general conversation about Machiavelli, Rich mentions that he knows Cromwell. Everyone present is shocked to learn that Cromwell has become Wolsey's secretary. Rich, alone, professes a liking for Cromwell. More manifests relief that he no longer needs to feel responsible for Rich now that he is in the company of Cromwell.

In the middle of the night More is summoned by Cardinal Wolsey, Henry's chancellor, a man of great wealth and power, both ecclesiastical and political. Wolsey is irritable and discourteous to More, keeping him standing instead of offering him a seat. Ostensibly, Wolsey wishes More to consider the request to the pope for Henry's divorce from Catherine; but in reality he wants More's support in getting the divorce. He has *The king's 'great* no moral restraints and sneers at More's suggestion that *matter' is* the king's council should be consulted before the letter *introduced.* is sent. More is extremely cautious and will not say what he thinks, even when the king's trumpet is heard, heralding his visit to Anne Boleyn, the king's future wife.

Wolsey faces More directly with the problem that Henry has no son, which the proposed divorce is all about (see Context and Setting). Wolsey, the complete

*Two men, two views.*

politician, cannot understand the principled Thomas More and becomes exasperated when he uses reasoned argument, which Wolsey calls 'plodding' (p. 12). When More states that the pope should decide on the validity of Henry's marriage, Wolsey reminds him, with some sarcasm, about the Wars of the Roses (see Context and Setting). Wolsey's point is that without a legitimate male heir for Henry (which Catherine had failed to produce) war would break out again and something practical must be done to prevent it. More believes that the actions of politicians should be guided by their consciences and not by what will get them their own way.

*A veiled threat.*

Wolsey is determined to find someone to carry out his will and threatens that if More won't, then Cromwell will, after he himself has gone: their parting words illustrate the bizarre situation in which the churchman is the Machiavellian and the politician is the Christian.

Although it is well past midnight, both Cromwell and Chapuys are close by, giving the impression that they are spying on More, trying to analyse the state of things through him.

More calls for a boat. The Common Man (as the boatman) comes forward. Cromwell interrupts his conversation with More, asking the boatman if he is licensed and pointing out that fares are fixed. Then, pretending to be surprised to see More, is fawning in his greeting. He wants to know whether More has acceded to Wolsey's request or not. The boatman's comment is a premonition of Cromwell's rise, which leads to More's decline.

*A threat from abroad.*

Chapuys, the Spanish ambassador, also knows Thomas More's movements, a fact of which More is aware. Chapuys will not ask More directly what the outcome of his visit to Wolsey was, but issues a threat from the

King of Spain, Charles V (nephew of Catherine), if the divorce goes through. More will not respond to Chapuys's questioning beyond agreeing that Wolsey and he parted 'amicably'. This is enough, however, for the ambassador to understand that More has not given the cardinal his consent to the divorce.

More's generosity is apparent in his payment of the boatman.

More's prospective son-in-law, William Roper, is with More's daughter, Margaret, when More returns home at 3am and has asked Margaret to marry him. More refuses to allow this on the grounds that Roper is a heretic, though Roper thought it was because More looked down on his family's status. An animated argument ensues about the state of the church. Roper expresses his opinions aggressively.

*Different views about the state of the church.*

*More avoids answering his family's questions.*

After Roper's departure on a borrowed horse, More avoids giving any information to Margaret about his meeting with Wolsey. More's wife, Alice, awakens and is annoyed that her horse has gone. More avoids answering his wife's questions about his meeting with Wolsey. Margaret asks if More would wish to be Chancellor if Wolsey fell and More admits that he would not.

*More is now chancellor.*

Time has passed. The Common Man comes forward and reads out from a book the information that More is now chancellor. Wolsey, accused of high treason, died on his way to his trial. Though the chancellor is regarded as a 'scholar and … a saint', it is also clear that he is still indifferent to political realities.

*Spying for the king.*

Cromwell is questioning Richard Rich about his new-found employment with the Duke of Norfolk and shows detailed knowledge of his duties. Cromwell, who had worked for Wolsey, now works for the king. Rich and Chapuys, the Spanish ambassador, who has burst in on their conversation, both want to know Cromwell's duties. Cromwell states that he is employed to spy and to translate the king's will into action.

The king's vanity is evident from his insistence on piloting the warship the *Great Harry* when it is launched. Chapuys corrects Cromwell's account of her armament, but is shocked to hear that Henry is going to speak to Thomas More about his proposed divorce. More's steward arrives and Chapuys, eager to question him, is reluctant to go. Cromwell has engaged the steward to spy on More, but his report confirms that More does not talk about the divorce.

Cromwell tries, unsuccessfully, to draw Rich into his web. More's steward gives a separate report about his master to Chapuys. The steward is making money giving them both useless information.

Rich now questions the steward about his conversation with the ambassador. The steward angers Rich by telling him which way Cromwell had gone before he was asked.

## COMMENT

*It is important in this play to read the stage directions which give strong indications about the manner in which people speak or react to situations.*

The introduction by the Common Man is meant to help us view the play in a realistic and natural way. More's gentle humour is immediately indicated in his apparently innocent question to the steward about the quality of the wine.

Rich's first remark 'every man has his price' gives an insight into his attitude to life in general and to his own in particular. More's disagreement with this attitude was followed to the letter in his own life. The characters of both men are being revealed to us right from the start.

More, who has a kind word for most people, finds it difficult to say anything about Cromwell, the complete Machiavellian, except that he has ability. Richard Rich seems set on following Cromwell's path rather than Thomas More's. His ambition is shown in the way he despises the role of teacher and his greed by taking the goblet, not for its beauty, but to sell it.

Another negative impression of Cromwell is conveyed by everyone's hostile reaction to the news that he has become Wolsey's secretary. The mention of Machiavelli and Cromwell almost in the same breath cannot be other than deliberate. The playwright is building up a picture of the man even before we see him on stage. The fact that Rich alone likes Cromwell is because he admires the way he works and would like to follow the same amoral path.

*Wolsey: churchman and politician.*

Wolsey is a hard-working pragmatist without scruples and wants Thomas More's approval to improve his chances of achieving what the king's wants. He has no personal consideration for More: he summons him in the middle of the night, does not offer him a seat at first and berates him for being late. He insults More by saying that, but for his conscience, he could have been a statesman. He sees the other man's reasoning as an encumbrance.

We have here a meeting of opposites in character and in temperament. The courteous Thomas More will make no comment on the king's philandering and, in spite of the seriousness of the business, never loses his sense of humour, as we see from his smile when Wolsey says there is much in the church that needs reformation and we suspect that More thinks reformation might begin with the cardinal. Furthermore, at the end of their meeting when Wolsey comments that More should have been a cleric, More replies with cutting humour: 'Like yourself, Your Grace?'

*Cromwell lives up to his reputation.*

Our poor opinion of Cromwell, created by the words and reactions of other characters, is unaltered by his attitude when he arrives on the stage: on the one hand, he is bullying and officious to the boatman; on the other, he is ingratiatingly servile to More. With people like him and Chapuys thronging the Thames at 3am, a definite atmosphere of intrigue and suspicion is created. The blackness of the river is an image of the kingdom. It is silting up because it is not free to go about its business, except at the centre of things where the waters are getting deeper.

Wolsey, Chapuys and later Henry himself all want Thomas More on their side, because his integrity is unquestioned, but More will not be open with any of them, in order to protect himself and his family.

William Roper is fiery and young, full of zeal for new causes, but goes the wrong way about winning More's permission to marry his daughter and insults his prospective father-in-law at the end of his visit. More's affection for Margaret is obvious and later in the play is shown to be greater than his love for his wife.

The brutality of the king can be discerned in the arraignment of Wolsey who had served him loyally, but had failed to arrange his divorce. The king's vanity is indicated in the way he takes the helm of his latest warship.

Cromwell openly admits to the Spanish ambassador that he is a spy and has taken over Wolsey's role as a tool of the king. This atmosphere of intrigue proves profitable for the Common Man, who pretends to spy for both, but gives away no secrets.

GLOSSARY

**Prologue** the introduction to, in this case, a play
**Old Adam** mankind before the Fall, now symbolically changed to the present state of general humanity by the addition of clothing (traditionally, Adam and Eve were said to be naked)

**Machiavelli** Italian author of *The Prince* which taught that rulers should use expediency rather than morality in their wielding of power. The 'Machiavel', based on a distorted view of Machiavelli, became a monster of the English stage

**Court of Requests** heard the cases of poor men in civil disputes

**Meg** Margaret

**stoop** swoop down on prey, used in reference to birds of prey

**Aristotle** Greek philosopher, quoted here by Rich to air his knowledge

**30 shillings** a large sum of money at the time; compare this with the 1½ penny fare (less than 1p today) for a boat from Chelsea to Richmond, a distance of several miles

**the Council** The Lords of the Council in the Star Chamber at Westminster is the full title. Although it was the king's council, and supposed to have considerable power, Wolsey often kept it in the dark about his activities

**the Yorkist Wars** the Wars of the Roses (see Context and Setting)

**Fisher** Bishop John Fisher, Bishop of Rochester, the only bishop who refused to swear the oath to the Act of Succession was made a cardinal by the pope in May 1535 and executed by Henry VIII the following month, a month before Thomas More

**Charles, King of Spain** the nephew of Catherine of Aragon, Henry's wife. Charles was also Emperor of Germany

***Dominus vobiscum*** the Lord be with you

**... *spiritu tuo*** and with thy spirit. Because More is distracted he only gives part of the response which, in full, is 'Et cum spiritu tuo'

**advocates** barristers

**Forgiveness by the florin** a reference to the corrupt church practice of selling indulgences to reduce the time a soul spent in Purgatory before reaching heaven

**florin** in modern coinage a ten-pence piece, but in the sixteenth century a valuable gold coin

**'Don't lengthen your prayers with *me*, sir!'** I don't want you praying for me

**Hampton** Hampton Court, the great house built by Wolsey and
subsequently taken over by Henry VIII

**'Are you coming in my direction, Rich?'** Are you going to work
with me to achieve the king's aims?

**Lent** Christian period of fasting and self-denial for the forty days
before Easter

**Confession** sacrament of repentance for sin

**Dominican** friar of the Order of St Dominic; friars travelled
about in the world, unlike monks who spent their lives in a
monastery

**'No man can serve two masters'** Christ's words, but here referring
to Cromwell and More

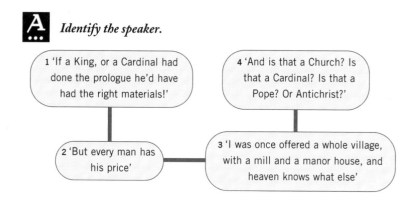

**A** *Identify the speaker.*

1 'If a King, or a Cardinal had done the prologue he'd have had the right materials!'

4 'And is that a Church? Is that a Cardinal? Is that a Pope? Or Antichrist?'

2 'But every man has his price'

3 'I was once offered a whole village, with a mill and a manor house, and heaven knows what else'

*Identify the person 'to whom' this comment refers.*

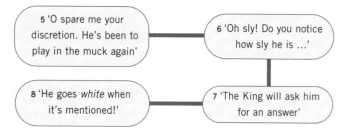

5 'O spare me your discretion. He's been to play in the muck again'

6 'Oh sly! Do you notice how sly he is ...'

8 'He goes *white* when it's mentioned!'

7 'The King will ask him for an answer'

Check your answers on page 86.

**B** *Consider these issues.*

a The role of the Common Man and its effectiveness in the play.

b What we learn of the character of Thomas More in Part I.

c How well More knows the people he is in contact with.

d Richard Rich's ambition and how Bolt informs us of this.

e Wolsey's attitude to Thomas More.

f The Machiavellian and Christian approaches to politics as displayed by Wolsey and More.

g The problem of the King's 'great matter': which is the hub of the whole play.

h Why everyone sought Thomas More's approval though their aims were different.

# ACT I

## PART 2 (PAGES 25–46)

*More shows his unworldliness.* The king is due to make a 'surprise' visit to Thomas More's house and all are in a panic because More cannot be found. Norfolk is becoming annoyed as the fanfare of trumpets announcing the king's arrival can be heard. More is eventually found attending Vespers. Only he behaves as if the visit is to be a surprise. Unlike the others, he is not even dressed for the occasion.

Henry arrives resplendent in cloth of gold and carries on the charade that the visit is a spontaneous act. Alice, confused, almost gives away the fact that they have been expecting him.

*The king's vanity is very obvious.* Conversing together in Latin, Margaret proves a better Latin scholar than Henry, who quickly changes the subject to that of dancing and wrestling. He is in great good humour and admits that More helped him to write his book on the seven sacraments of the Church, though More plays down his part in it. Everyone, except Henry and More, enter the house.

*Though friendly, the king is putting pressure on More.* More shows the king great deference, but makes the mistake of praising Wolsey's ability. Henry's mood immediately changes from friendliness to irritation. He claims that Wolsey failed to get his marriage annulled because he had ambitions to become pope. The king's agitation about 'the one thing that matters' cloaks a threat to More, though the king may not consciously intend it. He calms down for a moment, speaking of his experience of piloting the *Great Harry* that afternoon, before again broaching the subject of his divorce. More is definite in his refusal to accept the king's wish, much to Henry's annoyance, though Henry respects his chancellor's integrity.

More reminds Henry that it was a condition of his taking office that the king would leave him alone on *Both men's views* this issue. Henry seems genuinely to feel that he is *are based on the* living in sin with Catherine and the two men quote *Bible.* chapter and verse from the Bible at each other in their argument. More wishes to pass the problem over to the pope, but Henry will have none of it, seeing his lack of a surviving son as God's punishment for his sin. Henry knows the motivation of Norfolk and Cromwell in following him, but needs a man of integrity, like More, to bolster his cause.

On a lighter note, the king discusses the music played by his musicians. More astutely observes that it is the king's own composition and praises it, while claiming a 'deplorable' taste in music.

*Opposition to the* Henry reverts to his overriding concern and this time *king would be* the threat is overt, when he says that he will regard *high treason.* those who oppose his marriage plans as traitors.

More is now worried. His business done, the king departs abruptly without waiting for dinner. Alice More accuses her husband of upsetting the king and begs him to retain the king's friendship. More's humorous remarks do not console her. The impetuous Roper arrives and, against Margaret's wish, importunes More with a request for his opinion on whether he should enter Parliament or not. Just as More is considering

*A treasonable
outburst.*

that Roper's views on the church might be an asset to him in Parliament, Roper indulges in a tirade about the enemies of the church that could be construed as treasonable. As the king's first minister, More must not listen to treason, but he is not offended by Roper's insults as Alice is.

*Rich is very clearly
distrusted.*

Richard Rich arrives to a tepid reception by the family and feels uneasy. He warns More that Cromwell is gathering information on him and that Matthew, his steward, is supplying it. More prevents Matthew slipping away, but More knows that he is under observation and that, naturally, Cromwell would approach his servant. Rich warns of Chapuys's spying too. He is in some distress and feels hostility from the family. Once again he begs More to employ him, but he will not because he is unreliable. Rich leaves and all suspect that he is a danger to More. Roper wants him arrested, but More is a guardian of the law and will not act illegally. He lectures Roper on the value of the law and its ability to protect his daughter and himself but fails to mention his wife, which causes Alice distress.

More leaves the room but quickly returns to apologise to Roper for being harsh and proclaims, as they go up to supper, that the law will protect him. It is noticeable that he does not apologise to his wife. Alice wants to know why Cromwell is collecting information about him but More shrugs it off with, 'Someone somewhere's collecting information about Cromwell' (p. 40). The atmosphere in England is that of a police state.

The Common Man now becomes a publican, letting a private room to Cromwell and pretending to know nothing about anything.

*Cromwell finds a
willing accomplice.*

Rich enters the room and finds Cromwell flushed with success at his promotion to secretary to the council.

Cromwell begins to talk like Henry now. He is testing

*Rich admits his*
*weakness.*

Rich to see whether he can trust him. Rich admits
that he can be bought, that money is his god and
Cromwell immediately promises him the post of
collector of revenues for the York diocese. Rich has
passed the corruption test and Cromwell proceeds to
guide him in the principles of expediency. Rich
recognises his fall from grace and their thoughts turn
to Thomas More. Both acknowledge More's innocence
and integrity.

Cromwell now displays his knowledge of More and
Rich by asking questions about the goblet More gave
the younger man. He plans to use this to undermine
More's reputation, even though he has just
acknowledged that he is innocent. Rich is becoming
more corrupt with each piece of information he gives
Cromwell. He wants to know what the information is
for and Cromwell claims he hopes to frighten More
into complying with the king's wishes. Rich reminds
Cromwell of More's innocence and fearlessness.
Cromwell shows a sadistic streak by putting Rich's
hand in the candle flame to demonstrate how people
can be made to fear.

## COMMENT

*The king's visit*
*and abrupt*
*departure is a*
*source of tension.*

We see the simplicity of More's character when he
refuses to panic, like the rest of his household, before
the king's visit. Since the king is not supposed to be
expected, he behaves as though he does not know he is
coming by wearing unsuitable clothes and attending
Vespers. Putting God before the king is symbolic of the
pattern of his life and is the cause of his death. This is
the first and only time we see Henry on stage and we
learn about many facets of his nature. His vanity is
demonstrated by his attempting to show off his Latin
to Margaret. When this does not go according to plan,
he tries to score points by praising his own prowess at
dancing and wrestling, but shows some humility in

acknowledging More's help with his book. He is quick to anger and very determined, though he does seem sincere in his belief that his marriage to Catherine is sinful. His childlike wish for approval is shown when he asks More rather obliquely to comment on some music he had composed.

It is in this section that More begins to show concern for his own safety and we hear the word 'Traitors' (p. 34) applied to anyone who opposes the king. In his abrupt departure, Henry shows no concern for Alice's efforts to provide a feast for him. We see in this part of the play the friction between Alice and her husband about his defiance and the lack of understanding between them, which will persist until his death.

The fiery Roper has changed his beliefs again and speaks treasonably in defence of the church. More's integrity is apparent in his attitude towards Roper's remarks (p. 36). To Roper, everything is black and white, whereas More knows better and shows great confidence in the law. More has the perfect sailing image (p. 39) for Roper's concepts, for they change like the wind; but he shows a less caring attitude towards his wife than he does to his daughter, causing her sorrow.

*In Rich, Cromwell has a helper and ally.*

The moral downfall and political rise of Richard Rich is well and truly cemented at the end of Act I. As Rich again entreats More for employment, the audience may think that he wants to get close to More to spy on him. The family certainly see him as a danger. He is a willing victim of Cromwell, who corrupts him entirely at this point, as he sets a trap for Thomas More, even though both Cromwell and Rich have agreed that More is an innocent man. This is the depth to which Cromwell has sunk: for him the end justifies the means and no morality intrudes.

GLOSSARY

**Vespers** Evensong, a Christian service with singing of psalms

**Latin** the international language of Europe because of the dominance of Catholicism. It remained so long after the rise of Protestantism in the sixteenth century

**Your Grace's Book** Henry's book, *A Defence of the Seven Sacraments*, which some suspected Thomas More wrote for him; it was for this book that the pope granted Henry the title *Fidei Defensor* (Defender of the Faith)

**courtship** court manners and etiquette

**Leviticus** and **Deuteronomy** books of the Old Testament of the Bible, which contain opposite commands regarding a man marrying his brother's wife

**nice** scrupulous

**Moloch** Phoenician god to whom children, often the first-born, were sacrificed

## A ... Identify the speaker.

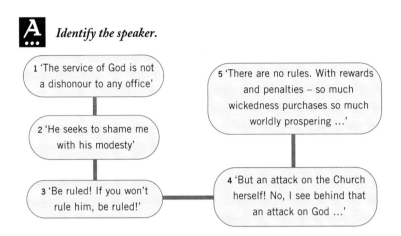

1 'The service of God is not a dishonour to any office'

2 'He seeks to shame me with his modesty'

3 'Be ruled! If you won't rule him, be ruled!'

4 'But an attack on the Church herself! No, I see behind that an attack on God ...'

5 'There are no rules. With rewards and penalties – so much wickedness purchases so much worldly prospering ...'

### Identify the person 'to whom' this comment refers.

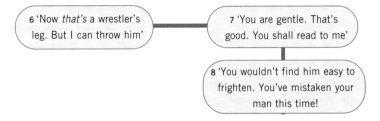

6 'Now *that's* a wrestler's leg. But I can throw him'

7 'You are gentle. That's good. You shall read to me'

8 'You wouldn't find him easy to frighten. You've mistaken your man this time!'

Check your answers on page 86.

## B ... Consider these issues.

**a** The contrast of naivety and subtleness in Thomas More's character.

**b** Notice the stage directions which so frequently give us an insight into character.

**c** The character of Henry, his faults and strengths.

**d** Henry's motive for divorcing his wife.

**e** Men's and women's views of the king's 'great matter' as demonstrated by Alice and Thomas More.

**f** Thomas More's sense of humour.

**g** The water and forest imagery and their effectiveness.

**h** The corruption of Richard Rich and the principles that govern the actions of Thomas Cromwell.

## Act II

### Part 1 (pages 47–74)

The Common Man tells us that two years have elapsed since the end of Act I and the Church of England is now established.

*The looming threat of the Act of Supremacy.*

More and Roper, as usual, are having an argument, this time about the wording of the Act of Supremacy. More has promised to resign as chancellor if the bishops agree to submit to Henry, but still feels he can be safe behind a wall of silence and the protection of the law. Roper and Margaret are both indiscreet and More has to warn them to keep their opinions to themselves.

Chapuys, the Spanish ambassador, enters repeating his initial words to claim some attention. His manner and language are ingratiating though More reacts with humour to his fawning, knowing why he has come. Chapuys shows himself to be utterly false, almost a caricature of simpering shallowness. Nevertheless, More is uneasy when Chapuys accuses him of being party to Henry's actions. The ambassador pinpoints the crux of the matter when he notes that Henry has moved from an injustice against his wife to an attack on religion itself. More's reaction is, as ever, cautious. Chapuys wants his support for a revolution to unseat the king.

*Norfolk brings unwelcome news.*

Norfolk makes a hurried entrance and Chapuys leaves with a lame excuse. Norfolk brings the news that the bishops have given in to the king and the Church of England has broken with Rome. This is the moment of truth for Thomas More, who wishes now to divest himself of his chain of office, causing Norfolk to rage against him. More gives Norfolk his reason, which echoes Chapuys's words: '… this is war against the Church!' (p. 52). There is a crucial difference between reform of the church and its destruction. More will not give his view on the validity of Henry's marriage to

Catherine, but he states his position on the apostolic succession of the pope. He then proceeds to give Norfolk a lesson in the necessity of caution. He now fears for his life.

*More resigns and his family face the consequences.*

The king accepts More's resignation and when Norfolk brings this news, More informs him of the danger of rebellion in the north. Cromwell, however, is already aware of this. Norfolk's parting jibe at More's patriotism brings an angry response (p. 54), but Roper is impressed.

More admits he was incapable of taking a different decision. Alice accuses him of treating his family cruelly, but Margaret springs to his defence. More reminds them all that he has never made a statement on Henry's divorce or Henry's claimed supremacy over the church and puts his faith in silence, demonstrating the importance of not giving them his views. Alice is upset at the drop in their standard of living. More shows consideration for the servants he must now dismiss.

Matthew, More's steward, is not loyal enough to continue to serve his master, who is genuinely sorry to see him go, even though he knows his steward's weaknesses. Likewise Matthew, as a realist, has no good opinion of himself.

*Cromwell prepares his trap.*

Norfolk wants More to be left in peace, but Cromwell is determined that he will swear loyalty to Henry's government. He seeks to undermine More's reputation by accusing him of bribery.

Rich enters and his too familiar attitude to Norfolk brings a stinging rebuff. Cromwell takes evidence from a woman who gave More the Italian silver cup which he gave away to Rich. Norfolk remembers the occasion clearly. Even Cromwell agrees that More's judgement was faultless and that he cannot make a case against More because he immediately gave the cup to Rich.

Undismayed by his failure, Cromwell intends to find some other way to discredit More and forces Norfolk to be part of the action by stating that it is the king's wish. It is not clear if this is true. Cromwell is determined to ensnare More, even if it means making a new law to do so.

Matthew, More's ex-steward, now seeks a post with Rich and argues his way into a job. Rich fears he will be insolent, as before, but nevertheless employs him. Matthew secretly despises Rich.

*A letter to trap the unwary.*

Chapuys visits More in his straitened circumstances. More is looking older now. Chapuys has brought a personal letter to him from the King of Spain but he will not accept it, for as a loyal subject his duty would be to take it to the king. Meanwhile people are putting their own interpretations on More's silence. Chapuys fails to trap him into giving support for an attempt to overthrow Henry.

The family is now so poor that having bracken to burn is a luxury. More refuses money sent him by the bishops even though they can now afford only the cheapest food.

More knows that Cromwell is out to get him but tries to reassure Alice that there is no danger. Roper enters:

*An unwelcome summons to Hampton Court.*

Cromwell has summoned More to Hampton Court to answer charges. Alice is in great distress. More retains his sense of humour and his confidence in his case, showing contempt for Cromwell, calling him 'the merest plumber' (p. 66).

On meeting Cromwell, who has Rich with him, More answers him with sarcasm, whereas Cromwell is sycophantic towards More. Rich shows his stupidity by writing down what they say before the business has begun. Cromwell does not like the word 'charges' and More immediately seizes on this and tells Rich to 'Make a note … There are no charges' (p. 67). Cromwell uses the king's name as he did with Norfolk but we have only Cromwell's word, no evidence that he is telling the truth.

Cromwell tries to trap More by linking him with the 'Holy Maid of Kent', who was executed for opposing Henry. Failing to achieve this, he then tries to make More betray himself about the pope's authority and Henry's marriage to Anne Boleyn. Again he is unsuccessful. More leaves and Cromwell outlines his designs to Rich.

*More tries to end a friendship.*

More cannot get a boat because the boatmen fear being associated with him, but Norfolk acknowledges their friendship. More explains that the love of God within him will not allow him to deny the authority of the pope. He cannot breach his inner integrity. More tries to start a row with Norfolk to make it easier for the duke to end their friendship, and warns him about the spiritual consequence of siding with the king.

*The net begins to tighten.*

Margaret and Roper enter bringing bad news. An Act of Parliament is to be passed about the king's marriage which will make taking an oath obligatory on pain of treason. More needs to know the exact wording before deciding how to act.

COMMENT

*The use of law.*

At the beginning of Act II, More explains to Roper the importance of exact wording when looking at the law. This is later to be the tactic of his defence. Notice how, at times of great distress, More indulges in humour. Chapuys's repetition of his opening words on entry is rather childish, as is his sycophantic reference to More as the English Socrates. In reality, More and Chapuys agree on the king's marriage and papal authority, but More cannot openly say so and he is, therefore, accused of being on Henry's side. Chapuys's excuse to Norfolk on leaving is as banal as his words on entry.

More has no option but to resign the chancellorship or support Henry in his arrangements for the church and his marriage. Alice cannot understand this. His stand is on integrity: being true to oneself. It is a time of intrigue and treachery, as is always the case when there is all to play for and all to lose.

Even in his fall from power, More has consideration for his staff and promises he will find positions for all of them despite Alice's protests. Though More knows Matthew's faults, it does not prevent him feeling affection for him.

We know Cromwell had astutely placed a spy among Chapuys's travelling companions on his journey to the north; now, he is scheming against More. Perhaps he has ambitions to succeed him as chancellor. The accusation of corruption against More fails because of Rich's stupidity in forgetting that Norfolk was present when Rich was given the cup. Norfolk is able to show that More gave away the bribe almost as soon as he had received it.

*The abuse of law.*

There is heavy **irony** (see Literary Terms) in Cromwell's reply to Rich that More's downfall must be brought about by law, since it will be by creating a new law that he traps him. Rich is a prime example of a weak man given power. He is frightened of Matthew even though he has authority over him.

More maintains that he has not taken a stand on the divorce, but has said that Henry has declared war on the church and the pope (p. 52). This gives an indication of where he stands, though his reaction to the letter from the King of Spain proves his loyalty to Henry. Throughout this stressful time, he retains his sense of humour.

Cromwell tells More (p. 69), as he had earlier told Norfolk (p. 60), what the king's wishes are. However, we have no means of knowing whether Cromwell is telling the truth or using the king's name to manipulate people for his own ends.

Norfolk's display of friendship for More in these circumstances is very moving. More gives a good example of why he acts the way he does – his inner self will allow no other way.

GLOSSARY     **Socrates** ancient Greek philosopher, Plato's teacher who, when condemned for corrupting the young with his ideas, accepted his fate and poisoned himself by drinking hemlock

**Erasmus** Dutch Catholic scholar and friend of More; he advocated church and social reform

## A Identify the speaker.

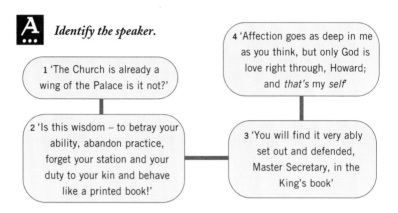

1 'The Church is already a wing of the Palace is it not?'

2 'Is this wisdom – to betray your ability, abandon practice, forget your station and your duty to your kin and behave like a printed book!'

3 'You will find it very ably set out and defended, Master Secretary, in the King's book'

4 'Affection goes as deep in me as you think, but only God is love right through, Howard; and *that's* my *self*'

## Identify the person 'to whom' this comment refers.

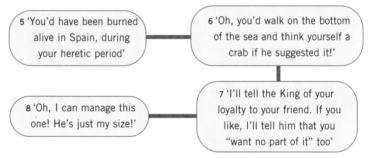

5 'You'd have been burned alive in Spain, during your heretic period'

6 'Oh, you'd walk on the bottom of the sea and think yourself a crab if he suggested it!'

7 'I'll tell the King of your loyalty to your friend. If you like, I'll tell him that you "want no part of it" too'

8 'Oh, I can manage this one! He's just my size!'

Check your answers on page 86.

## B Consider these issues.

**a** More's insistence on literal interpretation of the law.

**b** The character of Chapuys.

**c** The crucial difference, as More sees it, between reformation and destruction of the Church.

**d** Thomas More's statement about integrity.

**e** Alice's attitude to More's resignation.

**f** The rise of Cromwell and his corrupt practices.

**g** Thomas More's loyalty to the king and contempt for Cromwell.

**h** Norfolk's friendship for More in adversity.

**i** The use of law to ensnare More.

# ACT II

## PART 2 (PAGES 74–99)

*More confronts his interrogators.*

Thomas More is in prison and the Common Man, now acting as jailer, reads an abbreviated account of the future fates of Cromwell, Norfolk, Cranmer and Rich. More is woken to meet Cromwell, Norfolk and Cranmer, now Archbishop of Canterbury. Though initially irritated, More's humour shines through in mock reverence for his important visitors. He is limping and ageing. Presented with the Act of Succession, he refuses to swear to it, though he will swear to the legitimacy of Anne's children as heirs to the throne.

Cranmer then takes up the interrogation, asking whether More has any problem with the annulment of Henry's marriage to Catherine. More remains silent, except for rebutting Norfolk's accusation of insulting the king and council. Cromwell and More interpret 'justice' very differently. On hearing his request for more books, Cromwell displays his viciousness by refusing him books and family visits. He also wishes the jailer to inform on the prisoner and offers him a reward if he does, though the jailer wants nothing to do with the business. Norfolk objects when Cromwell orders Rich to remove More's books next morning. Cromwell retorts with a thinly veiled threat about the king's impatience.

From his behaviour, Cromwell is pondering whether to use the rack. He wants More's submission, not his death, because he knows that he, too, is vulnerable. He therefore allows More's family to visit him on condition that they try to persuade him to take the oath.

*More faces pressure from his family.*

The rack is there for the family to see. Amid a strained atmosphere, More shows more affection for his daughter than his wife. He resists Margaret's arguments that he could say the words of the oath but not mean them or that he is indulging in self-glorification, affirming that to take the oath would be a betrayal of his essential self. Margaret's greatest weapon is to tell him of their loneliness without him and the impoverished state in which they live. More is much moved by this. Fearing for his family, he begs them to leave the country, for he knows that he is doomed.

More's attitude to his wife is patronising and Alice is resentful. He begs his family to understand his struggle, but Alice is angry with him. More wants to share the food they have brought him with John Fisher, imprisoned close by.

The jailer declares that time is up and a scene of frenzied chaos follows as the jailer tries to usher the family away and they resist. It seems that, even in jail, More is being watched. The jailer says that he is just keeping out of trouble, like most of the population.

*More is brought to trial.* The trial of Thomas More begins with the Common Man being elected foreman of the jury. More is feeble from his deprivations and requests a chair. He is charged with high treason. Bishop Fisher has been executed that very morning on the same charge. The charge is the false one of denying Henry the title of Supreme Head of the Church in England. More's defence is that he has been silent on this subject and imprisoned for his silence.

Cromwell expounds at length upon the silence of Thomas More, who then corrects him with regard to the law; his interpretation of 'Silence Gives Consent' (p. 92) is the opposite of Cromwell's. The word 'conscience' is sneered at by Cromwell and provokes a scathing rejoinder from More. More's stubbornness is to Cromwell 'frivolous self-deceit', whereas to More it is 'respect for his own soul' (p. 92). Their hatred for each other is evident.

*The corruption of Rich is absolute.*

Rich is called to give false evidence that More denied Henry's title as Head of the Church. More rebukes Rich for his perjury and denies the accusation. The court is rigged; the trial a sham. More wishes to call Sir Richard Southwell and Master Palmer as witnesses, but, conveniently, they have both been sent to Ireland on the king's business. More sees this as proof of his innocence, for if he were guilty, they would have been called as witnesses by the prosecution to corroborate Rich's accusation. More makes a final disparaging remark to show his contempt for Rich and rejects Cromwell's last-minute offer of reprieve.

There follows another blatant denial of justice as Cromwell bullies the jury into reaching an instant decision without retiring for discussion. More is pronounced guilty. Even now, and still with a smile, More corrects the court on the matter of procedure.

*At last More can express his views.*

Having been condemned, More is free to reveal his opinion: it is that the king has not the authority in Parliament to take upon himself supremacy of the church, since it is a spiritual supremacy and the king has broken his coronation oath in so doing. More angrily accuses Cromwell of seeking his death because he will not accept the king's marriage to Anne Boleyn. The death sentence is then passed.

On his way to execution, More is met by his daughter, Margaret, whom he tries to comfort, and a callous woman, who accuses him of giving an unjust judgement against her, which he denies. He is kind, even to the executioner, and meets his death happily.

Cromwell and Chapuys go off together 'chuckling'. They are both politicians and live by compromise.

COMMENT     It is interesting to learn that of Cromwell, Norfolk, Cranmer and Rich, only Rich was not condemned to death. Rich had learnt the art of compromise to perfection. Norfolk, too, survived, but only because Henry died before signing the order for his execution.

*More remains unbowed.* Though More is physically deteriorating in prison, his sense of humour is as sharp as ever, as his mind and spirit prove to be during the trial. His courage and opposition to the king's will remain as strong as ever.

Cromwell seems to have few redeeming features and many nasty ones, which are again displayed when he deprives More of books and family visits. He believes that every man has his price, but he has over-priced, and so frightened, the jailer who will not cooperate.

Like Christ before Pilate, More responds with silence to Cranmer's questioning (p. 77). At every turn, More and his accusers are at loggerheads. In particular, he and Cromwell disagree on what 'justice' means and on the interpretation of 'Silence Gives Consent', as well as on the Act of Supremacy and oath of allegiance. Cromwell cannot stoop lower than to use More's family against him. England is a police state indeed when More and even the jailer are watched in prison. The rack is put where More can see it to torture his imagination, if not his body, with what might happen.

The keenness of More's mind is shown at the trial when he demonstrates that the prosecution's failure to

*More defends*
*himself with skill*
*and dignity.*

produce Southwell and Palmer, the other witnesses to what More said to Rich, casts doubt on Rich's evidence. During the trial, More is sufficiently composed to be able to instruct the court in the interpretation of the law and in court procedure. The trial itself is a mockery of justice, for More is condemned on the uncorroborated evidence of one man. More shows he is telling the truth by swearing an oath that he prays he himself might go to hell if Rich is telling the truth. The jury is bullied by Cromwell into giving the verdict he wants. More's unbowed spirit flares up in his contemptuous remarks to Cromwell and Rich and in his delivery of his true thoughts on the king's 'great matter.'

We should feel some compassion for Norfolk, who has to pronounce the sentence on his friend. It is the last thing he would have wished, yet he *is* party to the rigged trial. More's attitude to death is exemplary and totally in keeping with his certain belief in salvation. We hear his opponent, Cromwell, laugh once – after the execution.

GLOSSARY

guinea £1.05p in modern currency, although worth much more at the time in which the play is set

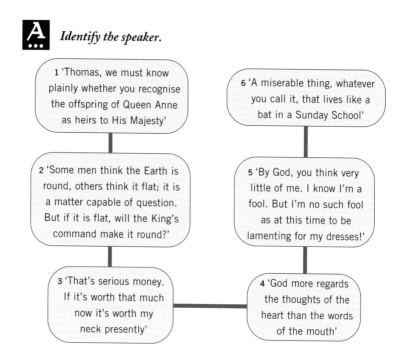

**A** *Identify the speaker.*

1 'Thomas, we must know plainly whether you recognise the offspring of Queen Anne as heirs to His Majesty'

6 'A miserable thing, whatever you call it, that lives like a bat in a Sunday School'

2 'Some men think the Earth is round, others think it flat; it is a matter capable of question. But if it is flat, will the King's command make it round?'

5 'By God, you think very little of me. I know I'm a fool. But I'm no such fool as at this time to be lamenting for my dresses!'

3 'That's serious money. If it's worth that much now it's worth my neck presently'

4 'God more regards the thoughts of the heart than the words of the mouth'

*Identify the person 'to whom' this comment refers.*

7 'You threaten like a dockside bully'

8 'Well, has Eve run out of apples?'

Check your answers on page 86.

**B** *Consider these issues.*

a The friction between Norfolk and Cromwell and how it is expressed.

b More's belief in the necessity to act according to conscience.

c The character of Cromwell.

d More's attitude towards his family.

e Alice's attitude to her husband's stand.

f More's final declaration of his belief and the way he accepts death.

# PART THREE

# COMMENTARY

## THEMES

### MORAL INTERGRITY

The theme of moral integrity is epitomised almost entirely in the person of Thomas More although Bishop John Fisher, who suffered the same fate for following his conscience, is also mentioned.

*Thomas More is unable to betray his inner self.*

'I will not give in because I oppose it – *I* do – not my pride, not my spleen, nor any other of my appetites but *I* do – *I*' (p. 72). More's expression of his selfhood is the cause of the central conflict in the play and is its most important theme. The soul or the inner essence of a person, that makes him what he is, is sacrosanct and may not be betrayed without destroying the person himself. More lived his life and lost it adhering to this principle. It becomes evident when he gives away to Rich the bribe he has just received. Wolsey recognises More's integrity, though he calls it a 'moral squint' (p. 10) and sees no need for conscience to affect actions. Chapuys, a scheming politician, acknowledges that More is a good man. The king himself respects More's sincerity when he vehemently informs Henry that he cannot accept the divorce.

To More there is a 'little … little, area where I must rule myself' (p. 35). Cromwell, of all people, confesses that More is an innocent man, although he views this as an obstacle to be overcome, rather than a quality to be treasured. Richard Rich has the same opinion of More.

*The bishops capitulate.*

The testing of More's resolve to stand by his principles begins in earnest when the bishops submit to the king, accepting the destruction, instead of the reformation, of the church. He defends the link with Rome because he believes the pope to be the successor of St Peter. '… I believe it to be true, or rather not that I *believe*, but that *I* believe it' (p. 53). His resignation from the office of chancellor, which plunged his family into poverty, was the only action he was capable of taking without compromising his conscience. 'To me it *has* to be, for that's myself!' (p. 71). He remains faithful to his conscience to the end, though assailed even by his own family, by imprisonment, by the terror of the rack openly on view by his cell and finally by the executioner.

## CORRUPTION

*The complete politician has no moral scruples.*

In this play, corruption is almost synonymous with politics and in Cromwell finds its greatest expression. To him a man's conscience is 'A miserable thing that lives like a bat in a Sunday School!' (p. 93). He has long ago decided to dispense with what gives a man moral dignity, preferring to follow a course of unremitting expediency.

As early as page 2, we find that, on Cromwell's advice, Rich has been reading Machiavelli, the arch-proponent of 'the end justifies the means'. Rich becomes as totally subservient to **Machiavellian** (see Literary Terms) principles as Cromwell and, therefore, utterly corrupt. It is hardly surprising, then, that the mention of Cromwell's name should cause unease in the More household.

Cardinal Wolsey is another who has sold his soul to the principle of expediency. He clearly does not see that More's conscience should have any bearing on his actions, 'your conscience is your own affair; but you're a statesman!' (p. 12). In this scene, the roles of cleric and politician are reversed: the politician is the man of honour and the cardinal the consummate Machiavellian.

Roper points out that corruption is rampant in the church and none is more corrupt than the cardinal, whose duty it is to eliminate it. When Wolsey falls, More is reluctant to succeed him as chancellor. After all, he does not possess the necessary cynical attributes of a political animal.

*More has no political ambition.*

Cromwell has so honed his nature to corruption that he is the perfect tool to ensure that Henry's wishes are obeyed, whatever the means. He corrupts Richard Rich by offering him lucrative posts and tells him plainly that wickedness provides worldly prosperity in equal portions. He is training Rich in subjecting all behaviour to what is convenient.

*Cromwell has no qualms about destroying an innocent man.*

Though he admits that Thomas More is an innocent man, he sets out to destroy his innocence by trying to force him to betray his principles for the convenience of the king. His attempt to trap More by showing that he accepted bribes is thwarted by Rich's incompetence. He also fails to trap More into saying that he supports the pope's authority in England because of More's cleverness. Cromwell uses any means at his disposal to weaken More's resolve, depriving him of books and family visits, even bribing his family to win him over to Henry's demands. In the end he can trap More only by corrupting the legal system, the very thing on which More relied for his security. The trial is rigged, false evidence given, the jury bullied and genuine witnesses got out of the way. It is the ultimate achievement of the unjust to corrupt the very source of justice.

The king has been corrupted by the great power he has, for he sees treason in all who cannot accept his views. His determination to marry Anne Boleyn is the principal cause of corruption among his subjects who, willingly or unwillingly, bow to his will. Even Norfolk, with all his affection for Thomas More, becomes part of the machinery of state that convicts and executes him and thus he, too, is tainted by the corruption. The pope himself is corrupt since, as a virtual prisoner of Charles V, his reaction to Henry's plea for a divorce is based not on moral grounds entirely but contains elements of political expediency. It is very obvious that corruption plays an immensely important role in this drama.

## LAW

*The validity of the law plays a central role.*

Laws of both church and state play a vital part in the unfolding of this play. All the conflict concerns the validity of law. Was the church law based upon Leviticus correct or should the passage in Deuteronomy be followed? Was the dispensation allowing Henry to marry Catherine valid or against the law of God? The validity of Henry's marriage to Catherine is the principal source of the major action in this play. Civil law is used by Henry and his creature, Cromwell, to suppress any opposition to his marriage to Anne Boleyn, just as Henry had used the charge of high treason to eliminate Wolsey when he failed to obtain an annulment of the king's marriage to Catherine. Cromwell's parody of lawfulness finally brings a just man, Thomas More, unjustly to his end.

*To More the law is sacrosanct.*

For More, the law is the protector of all who keep it. He puts his faith in the law as the instrument of justice, so that when Cromwell tells him he is threatened with justice, he can reply, 'Then I'm not threatened' (p. 79). 'Justice', however, means different things to each of them. In More's eyes, the law is straightforward and means exactly what it says, whereas morality may be clouded and unclear (p. 39). He will abide by the letter of the law in an effort to save himself.

*The law is for the protection of all.*

More's respect for law can be seen after he returns home from his visit to Wolsey, when he reprimands Alice for 'treasonable' words (p. 18) and Roper, too (p. 38). When Roper urges More to arrest Rich, he will not do so, for the law must be a safeguard for everyone, good or bad, until they break it. He would give even the Devil benefit of law, though Roper would cut down all the laws in England rather than allow the Devil their protection. More asks him, 'where would you hide, Roper, the laws all being flat?' (p. 39). The law's protection is for *all* so that each may be protected. More places his trust firmly in the law to save himself and his daughter. When Act II opens, the Church of England has been established by Act of Parliament. The Act of Supremacy proclaimed the king Head of the Church in England, 'so far as the law of God allows' (p. 48). What God allows is a matter of opinion.

Rich is anxious to ensure that More is trapped legally, but his words are at once twisted by Cromwell to mean they must find or make a law to destroy More (p. 61). For Cromwell, the law is an instrument of oppression, not protection.

*The law is used as an instrument of oppression.*

The Act of Succession required the taking of an oath accepting the children of Henry and Anne Boleyn as heirs to the throne of England. The implication of this, of course, is that Henry's marriage to Anne is lawful, whereas his marriage to Catherine was not. The precise wording of the oath is of the utmost importance to More, since it might be possible to take it without betraying his principles.

Though More accepts that Anne's children are the legal heirs to the throne, he is unable to take the oath required by the Act of Succession. Under Cranmer's questioning about the validity of Catherine's marriage, he maintains a silence which might indicate that this is his point of disagreement, but in law may not be so construed. The law states that 'Silence Gives Consent'. More's downfall is achieved by the corruption of true justice in a rigged trial.

The Common Man informs us how the law is to be used in the future to execute Cromwell and Cranmer and to condemn Norfolk. Although this, of course, is something that More will not live to know.

## STRUCTURE

The play, in two acts, is the straightforward chronological story of the hero, Thomas More, from the good times early on, through the dangerous period of his conflict with the king to the climax of his condemnation and execution.

The play is true to the historical facts. The Common Man introduces scenes and comments upon them in the nature of a **chorus** (see Literary Terms), speaking directly to the audience before donning some article of clothing and taking part in the action of the play. He also offers the audience information from outside the play. This so-called alienation technique, Bolt tells us, is meant 'to deepen, not to terminate,' our involvement in the drama.

*The stage directions help our understanding of the characters.*

The stage directions are quite explicit and give important clues to character and behaviour, which afford us greater insight into the author's intentions. The entire play revolves around Thomas More, who is present in almost every scene. Even when More is absent, in the scene in which Cromwell corrupts Rich, they are discussing how to find him guilty of taking bribes and so he has a direct bearing on the scene. The other characters are mainly defined in accordance with their relationship with More, and through their interaction with him we are given an understanding of his character. It is a well-constructed play, which holds the audience's attention at all times, despite the fact that the historical outcome is well-known. There are no **sub-plots** (see Literary Terms) or devices to draw the attention away from the main story.

*There is little action on stage.*

Though there are scenes of lively argument, the action on stage is generally static, apart from the wild struggle of More's family with the jailer in prison. We are given accounts of action off stage, however, when Henry tells us of the excitement of taking the tiller of the *Great Harry*, Norfolk exults in the glorious exploits of his falcon and Chapuys talks of his northern tour. Furthermore, we are drawn into the larger world of Europe with mention of Luther, Rome, the pope and Charles V of Spain.

The play has an alternative ending, used in the original London production, in which the Common Man advises people to keep a low profile if they want to stay alive.

# CHARACTERS

## THOMAS MORE

The central facet of More's character is his integrity, acknowledged by all, even his enemies. He advises Wolsey to show the Latin dispatch to the council, rather than hide it from them as Wolsey proposes to do and, in the same scene, states to the corrupt cardinal his belief that politicians only lead their country astray when they forsake their consciences. He stands out as a politician with principles, in contrast to the churchman with none, and refuses to support Wolsey.

He is incapable of flattery, which is confirmed by his wife, Alice, the best possible witness. More will not employ Rich because he knows he is unreliable and can

*Intelligent*
*Principled*
*Humorous*
*Courageous*
*Shrewd*
*Generous*

be bought. When members of his family want Rich arrested, More refuses to abuse his power, even though it puts him in danger and eventually brings about his death. He defends the rule of law to the bitter end. When a bribe is offered him, it has no effect on his judgement and he immediately gives it away.

As noted in Themes, More's integrity is commented on by Wolsey, who calls it a 'moral squint'; by Chapuys, the Spanish ambassador, who considered him a good man; by the king himself, who respects his sincerity; by Cromwell, to whom More's innocence is an obstacle; by Richard Rich, who agrees with Cromwell and, finally, by Alice, for whom he was 'the best man I ever met or am likely to' (p. 86). His integrity is so unshakeable that he will lay down his life rather than compromise his inner beliefs.

His sense of humour is evident a number of times throughout the play, even when the circumstances are most dire, though it sometimes turns into bitter **sarcasm** (see Literary Terms). More's second utterance in the play is tongue-in-cheek, as he asks his steward whether the wine is good, knowing that he has just been tasting it. He has only to smile at Wolsey's pompous statement about much in the church needing reform to condemn that prelate out of his own mouth. His parting words to Wolsey, when the cardinal says More should have been a cleric, are: 'Like yourself, Your Grace?'; another condemnation. The humour is gentler when Alice wants him to take a drink, remarking that colds attack important people as well as commoners (p. 19). His response is to warn her that she could end up in the Tower. Roper's self-important remark that his spirit is perturbed (p. 36) is greeted by More's suppressed grin and wide-eyed innocent questioning. He makes similarly impish remarks when he suggests Rich might feel the goblet he gives him is contaminated because it is a bribe and again when, grinning maliciously, he thinks he discerns a halo around Roper. More's humour takes on a sharper edge when Cromwell tells him that Rich will record their conversation. His sarcastic reply, 'Good of you to tell me, Master Secretary', implies that the conversation would normally have been recorded secretly. A further example of bitter **sarcasm** (see Literary Terms) is when More assumes the word 'conscience' is unknown to Cromwell. Even after he has been condemned, he can still raise a smile as he instructs Norfolk in court procedure.

More's loyalty to the king never wavers. He affirms this to the king himself when Henry visits the Mores' home in Chelsea. He will not hear treasonable talk even in his own home from members of his own family. More informs Norfolk about a possible revolt in the north and will not accept the letter Chapuys brings him from the King of Spain. He is condemned for high treason, but has never been disloyal. He makes play of breaking his friendship with Norfolk, but this is wholly artificial in order to protect the Duke and is really a display of loyalty towards him.

As a statesman, even an honest one, More needs a certain amount of shrewdness. He easily sees through Chapuys's pretence of visiting him to pay his respects as a brother in Christ and his reply is, indeed, down-to-earth. In the opening scene, he knows Matthew has been at the wine. With great caution he avoids answering the questions of his family about the visit to Wolsey. He will make no comment to Wolsey about the king's visit to Anne Boleyn or on the content of the Latin dispatch. He refuses the money offered by the bishops, even though his family are in great need of it. More will not disclose his thoughts on the Act of Supremacy, even to Roper in his own house and he warns Roper and Margaret to be discreet. More understands Cromwell's deviousness and political pragmatism and, therefore, would not wish him to be chancellor, but his comment on Cromwell is merely, 'He's a very able man' (p. 3). He know that Chapuys's sources of information are reliable and, on a lighter note, sees through the king's little ploy about his own musical composition. More is aware that Cromwell is questioning his servant about him and may even know that his servant is reporting useless information, since he does not dismiss him. More instructs Norfolk on the necessity of caution in their world of intrigue and espionage. He thoroughly understands the character of Richard Rich and clearly explains to him that a political life would corrupt him. The events of the play confirm the soundness of this judgement.

On first being arraigned before Cromwell, who refers to the charges as 'some ambiguities of behaviour' (p. 67), More is quick to demand that Rich make a note of the fact that there are no charges. His shrewdness is more than a match for Cromwell during interrogation. He stakes his security, and so his life, upon the letter of the law and on silence, which the law will interpret in his favour, whenever he finds himself unable to agree with the king's edicts. More proves to the court that the evidence against him is false because Southwell and Palmer, the other witnesses of what was said, are not in court as witnesses for the prosecution. Their absence is, at the very least, circumstantial evidence that Rich is lying.

Thomas More's courage is unquestioned. He tells Henry firmly, and to his face, that he cannot go along with his divorce. He tries to argue the biblical case on which the church's judgement rests, though the king will not listen. In prison, he will not take the oath demanded by the Act of Succession, nor say why he will not. Finally, he faces execution with great fortitude, even 'blithely', and has a kind word for his executioner.

Thomas More's disposition is, on the whole, patient and kind, though he can be roused to anger and sarcasm (see Literary Terms), the last of which has already been noted. Richard Rich affirms that, '... everyone's affable *here*' (p. 3), meaning in the More household. Matthew, the steward, tells us that his master will give anything to anybody and that he should practise keeping things for himself. More shows patience with Roper when he is ranting against the church after More's visit to Wolsey, until his anger flares when Roper calls the pope Antichrist (p. 17). More is understanding when Matthew decides to leave his service and shows real affection for him. More does not appear resentful when Wolsey summons him in the middle of the night and keeps him standing. Though Wolsey is highly irritated and speaks to him in an insulting way, More maintains his equanimity. Although fully aware that Cromwell is trying to get information about him from Matthew, More does not blame his steward in any way. When More is called before Cromwell, his first thoughts are not for his own safety but to console Alice. Although More cannot honestly recommend Rich to anybody, he brings him to the attention of Norfolk and leaves it to the Duke to decide whether or not to employ him.

More has strong religious faith; he prays that Henry and Catherine should have a son and admits to Wolsey that he should like to govern the country by prayers. It is the strength of this faith that enables him to go to his death with composure.

Although the nature of Thomas More is heavily weighted in favour of good, we are told in the stage directions at the trial that he and Cromwell hate each other. As we have seen, he is certainly capable of scathing remarks to Wolsey, Cromwell and Rich. Nor can he resist a last, pitying comment to Rich about selling his soul for Wales. He uses straight talking when refusing to allow Roper to marry Margaret and is irritated when Chapuys fawningly compares him to Socrates, which he glosses over with a joke. His worst fault would appear to be his attitude to his wife, Alice, who certainly comes second to his daughter and is treated in a patronising way, particularly when More is in prison. She knows she is second best and feels that her husband is being cruel to his family by not taking the oath. Norfolk also says that he has always known that More has a cruel streak in his nature.

## THOMAS CROMWELL

*Scheming*
*Bullying*
*Sadistic*
*Pragmatic*
*Ruthless*
*Ambitious*

Before Thomas Cromwell appears on stage we have already built up an opinion of him from others' comments about him and their reactions when his name is mentioned. In answer to More's question, Richard Rich, guiltily and with much hesitation, admits that it is Cromwell who has advised him to read Machiavelli; thus, we glimpse Cromwell as a follower of pragmatic political thought. Thomas More's reaction to Cromwell's name being introduced is cautious and repeated, 'He's a very able man' (p. 3), which immediately raises suspicion in our minds, because something has evidently been left unsaid. Norfolk causes consternation among More's family by announcing Cromwell's promotion to secretary to Wolsey. Alice, Margaret and More himself are aghast at the news. Rich, alone, professes to like Cromwell, while Alice retorts that Rich must be the only man in London who does. Cromwell is, then, almost universally disliked. More confesses to Wolsey that he has no wish to be chancellor, but would be prepared to take it on rather than see Cromwell in the post.

On his first appearance in the play, Cromwell shows an officious, bullying attitude to the boatman, while being sickeningly ingratiating towards More. His appearance on the river bank at nearly three in the morning can mean only that he is spying on More. The boatman's comment about Cromwell is ominous, 'The coming man they say, sir' (p. 14).

Cromwell tells us that he is 'The King's Ear' (p. 21) and the one who makes sure the king's will is obeyed. He seems to know every detail of Rich's employment with Norfolk, but, on the other hand, the information he has about the *Great Harry* is inferior to the Spanish ambassador's, which calls into question the efficiency of his non-spying activities. He is bribing Matthew, the steward, for information about More, even though all he receives in return, the steward says, is useless information. His comment to Norfolk, 'This isn't Spain' (p. 61), shows that he knows word-for-word what had been said in More's own house. Cromwell is ambitious and admits it to Chapuys.

Thomas Cromwell is astute enough to recognise that he can forge Rich into a willing tool. Although unsuccessful at the first attempt, he later wins him over with the promise of the lucrative post of collector of revenues for the York diocese.

Cromwell arrogantly speaks to Rich in the terminology of the king and expounds to him his political opinion that expediency should direct behaviour, that religion is an encumbrance and that wickedness buys success. To Cromwell, behaviour is directed by convenience: he is the complete **Machiavellian** (see Literary Terms). He at once sets out to trap More on a charge of bribery, though he knows it to be false. He has no scruples and corrupts Rich for the purpose of destroying More. Act I ends with Cromwell sadistically holding Rich's hand in a candle flame.

At every opportunity, Cromwell seeks to humiliate Norfolk by pointing out his lack of wit and learning. He is determined to attack More, though Norfolk wants him to be left alone. This could be due to jealousy, or zeal for the king's cause, or perhaps both. He underestimates the strength of More's will and expects him to submit. Cromwell is a bully and this trait may play a part in his determination to oppress More, once he has the power to do so. He uses the king's favour to threaten Norfolk if he does not cooperate in the attack on More. We have no evidence that Cromwell is telling the truth when he issues the king's commands.

Cromwell proves himself no match for Thomas More when interrogating him about the Holy Maid of Kent or on the extent of the pope's authority. In the king's name, he questions More about his thoughts on Henry's marriage to Anne, a point the king had specifically promised More he would not pursue. This casts doubt on whether Cromwell is acting on the king's wishes or his own.

There are no depths to which Cromwell will not stoop to defeat More. He uses his family, takes away his books, plays with the rack wondering whether to use it, misuses the law and resorts to perjury. At the end of the trial Cromwell is again the bully, forbidding the jury to retire to consider their verdict. His cruelty is apparent in the casual way he mentions Bishop Fisher's execution on the same charge. In arguing points of law, Cromwell is still inferior to Thomas More at the close of the drama and he reveals a hatred for him, which only More's death will satisfy. True to his **Machiavellian** (see Literary Terms) principles, he removes the witnesses that could deny the truth of Rich's testimony, thus ensuring More's death.

The way in which Cromwell links arms with Chapuys after More's execution and their chuckling exit denotes that Cromwell and his enemy, the Spanish ambassador, see themselves engaged in a game in which morality and human decency have no part.

## RICHARD RICH

*Weak*
*Untrustworthy*
*Mendacious*
*Greedy*
*Corruptible*
*Ambitious*

Richard Rich gives the key to his character with his first utterance, 'But every man has his price!' He is a man who can be bought. On Cromwell's recommendation he has been reading Machiavelli's *The Prince* which advised rulers to govern pragmatically rather than ethically. Thomas More's steward is contemptuous of him from the start. More himself knows he is untrustworthy and bribable and for that reason will neither employ him nor recommend him for employment. Rich, however, has ambitions and despises the post of teacher that he has been offered. His very name (which was his real one) betokens his aim in life. Having no integrity of his own, he is sceptical when More tells him he took office under orders.

He is a young man who likes to make a show of being knowledgeable, as he does when talking about Socrates. He professes to like Thomas Cromwell, the ultimate politician, when everyone else dislikes him. Rich accepts the gift of a goblet from More, not because it is beautiful or useful, but to sell it. He later cooperates with Cromwell in an attempt to destroy More's reputation with this same goblet. More's steward again comments unfavourably on Rich. No one has yet had a good word to say about him.

Despite his ambition and admiration for Cromwell, Rich, at first, will not follow him and is furious when the steward, who understands him, assumes that he will. When Roper is introduced and hears Rich's name, it is obvious that he has heard nothing but ill of him. Rich is nervous at meeting Thomas More's family which might be because he feels they dislike him, but perhaps he is planning to spy on them for Cromwell. Whatever the reason, Rich seems to have a guilty conscience. The family see Rich as a danger to More and Roper wants him arrested.

At his meeting with Cromwell, Rich is finally and thoroughly corrupted, admitting that he would do almost anything for money. He knows that he has fallen from grace and from now on his only direction, morally, is down, yet he perceives innocence in Thomas More and warns Cromwell that he has underestimated him. When Cromwell puts Rich's hand in the candle flame, he is demonstrating that he can now do what he likes with him. The fact that Rich stays with him proves it to be true.

Cromwell and Rich plan to destroy More's reputation by accusing him of taking bribes. This fails because Rich has forgotten that Norfolk knew about the goblet and could prove that More gave it away as soon as he had received it. Rich is not yet practised enough in evil; he wants to ensnare More legally.

Rich is a weak man and worries that Matthew will not be sufficiently deferential if he employs him as steward. He is also rather silly when More is interrogated the first time: Cromwell has to stop him writing down all the initial pleasantries.

Rich has no sense of occasion. When Cromwell is preoccupied with breaking down Thomas More's resistance, Rich can think only of pestering him for promotion to the post of Attorney-General for Wales. Needless to say, Cromwell ignores him. In order to gain this 'honour', Rich shows just how deeply corrupt he is by giving false evidence in court against More. In taking the oath to tell the whole truth, he hesitates to say, 'So help me, God' and has to be prompted by Cranmer (p. 93). There is an iota of conscience still to be overcome, it seems. He swears that More denied the Act of Supremacy when speaking to him in jail. Thomas More's words convey the utter contempt he has for Rich's perjury, a contempt restated when More finds Rich's perjury has secured him the post of Attorney-General for Wales.

There is a dreadful, but historically accurate, **irony** (see Literary Terms) here. We are shown the depths to which Rich has sunk. But we also know from what the Common Man has told us that Rich, for all his weakness, becomes Lord Chancellor and dies in his bed. His ability to compromise has ensured worldly success and security.

## THE DUKE OF NORFOLK

Thomas Howard, Duke of Norfolk, is a close friend of Thomas More and his family. This is obvious in the way he and Alice argue about his falcon's capability. He is not an educated man. When he says he has not much use for Aristotle, we get the impression that he knows nothing at all about him. He has heard of Machiavelli's 'nasty book', but has obviously not read it.

He is considerate enough to take Richard Rich home to his (Rich's) lodgings and to employ him in his library without any recommendation from More. His manner is down-to-earth and his language **colloquial** (see Literary Terms): 'That's where the Cardinal crushed his bum!' (p. 9).

The duke is solicitous for Thomas More's welfare; hence the panic when More cannot be found moments

*Bluff*
*Honest*
*Loyal*
*Kind*
*Fiery*
*Unsophisticated*

before the king's 'unexpected' visit. He is worried that More's career will be affected by it. He displays no airs and graces but speaks bluntly, telling him off for not being dressed suitably to greet Henry.

Norfolk has a fiery temperament, and when More wants to divest himself of his chain of office explodes into expletives and rails at More for being so calmly rational. His plain-speaking and volatile nature again manifests itself as he departs saying he is glad More still has a trace of patriotism left in him.

He does his utmost to protect More from Cromwell's viciousness. He advises Cromwell that More be left alone, since he has not spoken against the king. He assures Cromwell of More's loyalty. The duke's anger flares when Cromwell accuses More of taking bribes, although to him More's behaviour is at times that of a crank. Norfolk triumphantly destroys Cromwell's bribery case against More by remembering the incident and the date it happened. He does not suffer fools gladly and is scathing to Rich when he becomes over-familiar with him.

Cromwell forces the duke to cooperate with him in the prosecution of his friend, Thomas More, by saying it is the king's wish. He is also made aware that his private conversations with More at his friend's house have been reported. He is open to More about his new role as prosecutor, yet professes his friendship for him in an emotional scene. Nonetheless he becomes so enraged by More's insults, thrown at him in a contrived quarrel, that he strikes out at him.

The duke is a good man and shares with Thomas More a hatred of Cromwell and his tactics, which is apparent whenever they are together. He is not highly intelligent and has difficulty at times in following More's reasoning. He does not know in his own mind whether

Henry's marriage is lawful or not but follows the decisions of those whom he respects.

Regardless of the harm it might do him, Norfolk cares about More to the end. He shows his consideration by ending the interview when he sees More's weariness. He objects when Cromwell orders his books to be removed and offers More a drink before his execution. It seems that the duke does not realise that the trial is rigged, because he asks Rich who made the statement. Unlike Cromwell, he wants the jury to retire to consider their verdict in the proper manner.

Altogether, Norfolk is a blunt, open, larger-than-life character who has no guile in him, but is trapped into becoming part of the machinery of state that will execute his friend.

**ALICE MORE**

Alice More, Thomas's second wife, is a robust, uninhibited woman, who says exactly what she feels, whether or not it is comfortable for her audience to hear. Her nature is similar to Norfolk's, and we see her first arguing with the duke and pouring scorn on his boasts about his falcon. She soon sees off the steward for being too admiring of Margaret, More's daughter (her step-daughter).

We know she is uneducated, for her husband offers to teach her to read. Her personality is strong and her language direct. She is not without snobbery, however, her response to Cromwell's appointment as Wolsey's secretary is: 'A *farrier's* son?' (p. 7).

*Blunt*
*Uneducated*
*Brave*
*Sensitive*
*Loving*

On a number of occasions she shows her impatience with More: with his dishevelled appearance on the king's visit; about the way he has upset the king on the same visit; on the fall in their standard of living and, with justification, at his patronising attitude on her visit to prison.

She understandably resents the fact that Thomas is concerned for his own and his daughter's safety, but makes no mention of hers. She shows some bitterness, accusing More of behaving cruelly and turns on Margaret, too, with biting **sarcasm** (see Literary Terms) when his daughter comes to his defence. Though she knows she comes second-best to Margaret in Thomas's eyes, she loves him and is concerned for his safety. She worries about Cromwell's ability to endanger him and in prison describes More as the best man she has ever met or is likely to meet.

She does not suffer fools gladly and tells Roper, with an oath, that she would have him whipped if she had the authority, for the way he has insulted her husband. Her impetuosity declares itself again when she echoes Roper's demand that Rich be arrested. Alice is honest and brave, never hiding her feelings. Her greeting to her husband in prison is cold because she is annoyed with him for bringing deprivation on them all, but it is quickly followed by the declaration of her feelings for him and the challenge to anyone who wishes to know her opinion of King Henry and his council.

Her final exit is wonderfully characteristic: she imperiously casts the jailer's hand from her, verbally abuses him and threatens him with vengeance, then makes a dignified departure.

MARGARET
*Intelligent*
*Well-educated*
*Loyal*
*Loving*
*Patient*

Margaret More, More's favourite daughter, is the only one of his children to appear in the play. She is intelligent and well-educated, as Henry finds to his chagrin when he tries to impress her with his command of Latin. Margaret tries to be a moderating influence upon her fiancée, William Roper, with little success. Like Alice, she fusses over her father's appearance when the king is due to visit them. When her father accuses

Roper of changing with the wind, she jumps to his defence.

She shares with Roper a tendency to be indiscreet and has to be warned by her father, who does not condemn them but tells them they are either idiots or children in their ignorance of the world. Margaret has immense respect for her father and is outraged when Alice accuses him of being cruel. But she also supports her step-mother, putting her arm around her waist and agreeing with her that More should take the money offered him by the bishops. Her love for her father is so great that she takes an oath to try to persuade him to swear the oath of allegiance to the Act of Succession and does her best to persuade him that he should do so. As More goes to his death, Margaret flings herself upon him in a final farewell.

## WILLIAM ROPER

William Roper becomes the husband of Margaret More but has constant and vehement arguments with his father-in-law, Thomas More. He is young, self-righteous, immature, intolerant and filled with religious zeal. We see him first, full of ardour for the views of Luther, with nothing but abuse for the church, going so far as to accuse the pope of being Antichrist. His views are far from stable, though, and he later becomes more tolerant of Rome, describing Henry's reformation as an attack on the church and an attack on God.

*Immature*
*Self-righteous*
*Arrogant*
*Vain*
*Indiscreet*
*Opinionated*

He is impatient in the extreme and selfishly considers his own needs before others', having no sense of timing whatsoever. At 3am, when More returns from seeing Wolsey, he is there asking for his daughter's hand in marriage. Just after Henry leaves More's house, Roper demands, despite Margaret's objection, More's advice on whether he should enter Parliament. He is clearly quite insensitive and unaware of the tensions caused by the king's visit.

Roper does not hesitate to hurl insults at More, calling him corrupt and a flatterer. He is also indiscreet, and More has to warn him that he (More) must not hear treason spoken. Like Hamlet, he dresses in black to draw attention to himself and make a symbolic statement. He even walks up and down to make sure he is noticed.

He finds More's resignation from the chancellorship impressive, but even then seems unable to grasp why More has done it, calling it a 'gesture'. This tallies with his advice to the imprisoned More, that he should take the oath and come out. He shows genuine fear for More's well-being when he observes the rack in prison, and makes a spirited attempt to distract the jailer in order to win a few more minutes for his family's visit to Thomas More.

## THE COMMON MAN

*Shrewd*
*Self-serving*
*Worldly*
*Knows his limits*

The Common Man is employed in a variety of roles but remains the same character. He is narrator, commentator and actor as the situation requires.

He is a man of the world who knows the art of self-preservation. He has no high opinion of himself. At the opening of the play, he admits he is not equipped to introduce 'Kings and Cardinals' with their superior intelligence and eloquence, but his comments upon characters fulfil an important purpose. He tells us, for instance, that Thomas More is overgenerous; as More's steward, he is contemptuous of Richard Rich. As the boatman, he is used to demonstrate More's generosity.

He fills in gaps in the information we need, as when he announces Wolsey's death and the appointment of

Thomas More as chancellor. He even gives an objective assessment of More's character at the same time.

As Thomas's steward, he is cunning enough to give Chapuys and Cromwell unimportant information for money. He is wise enough, however, not to get out of his depth by indulging in any real espionage and he acknowledges this.

The Common Man's defence of himself for not taking any stand is that he could not possibly be expected to follow the thoughts of a man who is so 'deep' as Thomas More, but the accompanying wink shows us his real intention is self-preservation. He uses the same technique when, as innkeeper, he claims to have no understanding of anything, to such a degree that Cromwell becomes suspicious.

At the beginning of Act II, the Common Man bridges the gap in time between the two acts and tells us about the establishment of the Church of England. Later, he gives information about the future fate of characters who are on the stage.

Self-interest is also a motivating force. When Thomas More falls from power, he will not continue to serve him for a lower wage, preferring to enter the service of Richard Rich, whom he despises.

The Common Man lives on his wits and it is his craftiness that dupes Rich into employing him. His suspicious mind even causes him to think that More is trying to keep him as steward for less money. There is an element of guilt in his explanation of the situation, because More has just insisted that he will miss him.

As the jailer, his character does not change. His main aim in life is to keep out of trouble by pretending not to understand what is going on. This is what most people in the country were endeavouring to do at the time.

It is in keeping with his title of Common Man, encapsulating in his character what is common to us all.

## CARDINAL WOLSEY

*Machiavellian*
*Ambitious*
*Intelligent*
*Irritable*
*Pompous*
*Ill-mannered*

Though Cardinal Wolsey appears in only one scene, he is at the heart of the problem of the king's divorce and, in confronting More with it, his character is revealed to us. He has the authority to call an important man like Thomas More to his house in the middle of the night and then complain irritably that he is late. He rudely leaves More standing and pushes the paper across the table, instead of handing it to him. He is both bad-tempered and ill-mannered.

He is amazed that More believes Wolsey should be open with the king's council, seeing it as a fault in More, since it was Wolsey's practice to act independently of the council. He prefers what he calls 'common sense' (that is 'expediency') to the 'moral squint' (p. 10) of honesty.

He continues to berate More bad-temperedly when he answers Wolsey's questions cautiously, calling him a 'plodder' (p. 10). When Henry's trumpet is heard, he sneers at More's avoidance of comment and in his bull-at-a-gate fashion says, 'He's been to play in the muck again' (p. 11). It might be interpreted from this remark that Wolsey believes in the validity of Henry's marriage to Catherine, which he is doing his utmost to destroy, since he shows disapproval here of Henry's affair with Anne Boleyn.

Wolsey's impatience shows by the way he grips More's shoulder with some violence. He is down-to-earth and very direct, demanding to know what More would do to solve the king's problem of having no male heir.

Although Wolsey tells More that they are alone, he startles him by asking suddenly and very loudly, whether he wants a change of dynasty. The implication is that somebody is taking notes of their conversation. Wolsey ridicules More's reliance on prayer alone to resolve the problem of the king's marriage and when he tries to use reason against Wolsey's scheme, the cardinal dismisses his argument as 'plodding' (p. 12).

Wolsey plans to put pressure on the pope to make a political rather than an ethical decision on Henry's marriage to Catherine. As More refuses to be party to his scheming, Wolsey belittles his reliance on his conscience and warns that the 'Yorkist Wars' (the Wars of the Roses) will return unless something is done.

Wolsey is a pompous man, sermonising on the need for reform in the church but implying not until the king has a male heir. More's smile tells us he knows just what a hypocrite Wolsey is. Though he has failed to drag More along the path he has taken, the cardinal is wise enough to suggest to the king that More and not Cromwell should succeed him. Wolsey's final words are hostile to More and hypocritical in supposing that Wolsey's will coincides with God's. Wolsey's remark that More should have been a cleric leaves him open to the rejoinder, 'Like yourself, Your Grace?' (p. 13).

We see a determined, ruthless politician in clerical garb, pouring scorn on conscience and Christian values; a rude and arrogant pragmatist, who indulges in priestly sanctimoniousness when it suits him, but is intelligent enough to choose his successor wisely.

HENRY VIII
*Vain*
*Irascible*
*Forthright*
*Bullying*
*Shrewd*

Henry, too, appears in only one scene, but his presence and his menace pervade the whole play. The king's problem is posed forthrightly by Wolsey: the king needs a male heir to prevent internecine strife recurring in the realm and his wife, Catherine, is unable to provide one.

The king is a vain man: his clothing is cloth of gold; he

strives to impress with his knowledge of Latin, his prowess in music, dancing and wrestling; his taking command of the *Great Harry* is a source of much pride. However, he is humble enough to acknowledge Thomas More's part in the writing of his book on the Seven Sacraments.

Henry seems to be genuinely fond of More as well as admiring him, but his temper is quickly aroused when More praises Wolsey's ability. He has difficulty controlling his agitation and the subject of this agitation, his divorce from Catherine, contains a hidden threat to his new chancellor. His exasperation at More's inability to agree to the divorce is tempered by his respect for him.

The king really seems to believe that God is punishing him for marrying his dead brother's wife by denying him a son and that he is living in sin with Catherine. He does not want to hear any counter-argument though, which might mean that he has some doubts.

Henry is a good judge of men. He recognises the character of Wolsey and the reasons why Norfolk and Cromwell follow him, but most of all he understands and respects Thomas More's sincerity and that is why he wants his support. The king is a very determined man and warns More that he will allow no opposition to the annulment of his marriage. He promises that he will not force More to deal with the problem, a promise that proves hollow.

An early sign of what is to come, and evidence of Henry's determination, is the way he brands as traitors all those who say that Catherine is his wife. The Act of Succession, the Act of Supremacy and the oath of allegiance show the king's resoluteness in compelling his subjects to bow to his will. The king has acted against the law of God in making himself supreme over the church and in casting aside his true wife for the sake of expediency, as Thomas More asserts after the verdict of 'guilty' has been pronounced.

**CHAPUYS**
*Devious*
*Fawning*
*Insincere*
*Callous*
*Corrupting*

Chapuys, the Spanish ambassador, is a purely political animal. We first meet him as More is returning from seeing Wolsey at Hampton Court. Without asking direct questions, he tries to wheedle out of More what has occurred at the meeting and seems satisfied with the answer he assumes he has got. His sources of information are excellent: he knows more about the *Great Harry* than Cromwell and he also knows the king's movements.

He uses bribery to obtain information from Matthew, More's steward. His attitude to More veers from the fawning and nauseous, to the threatening when saying what the King of Spain will do if his aunt, Catherine of Aragon, is discredited. He uses any means to achieve his ends: flattery, threats or friendliness. He is attention-seeking and ingratiating in the most obvious way when he twice refers to Margaret and Roper as potential saints and addresses More as the English Socrates. His sincere insincerity is stretched to the limit. Yet he has the effrontery to accuse More of corruption, by implying that he has aligned himself with the king's policies.

Chapuys makes two clumsy attempts to turn More into a traitor: encouraging him to spark off a revolt in the north and trying to give him a letter from the King of Spain. He may feel he understands the minds of politicians but the honesty of Thomas More has him completely confused.

His last exit, chuckling and arm-in-arm with Cromwell, sums up his insincerity and expedient attitude to life.

### THOMAS CRANMER, ARCHBISHOP OF CANTERBURY

Cranmer appears only briefly. He is a fussy man and
irritates More by twice questioning the state of his soul.
He is a tool of the establishment, oppressing people and
forcing them to do his will on peril of their souls, as he
does with the jailer, attempting to compel him to
inform on More. He is upset when More does not wish
him to accompany him to the scaffold, perhaps seeing it
as a comment on his character as, may be, it is.

## LANGUAGE & STYLE

The play is written in simple, modern, **colloquial prose**
(see Literary Terms), sometimes strung with oaths from
earlier times. People of eminence and the Common
Man do not have different styles of speech. There are
no long passages and the short interaction of
conversation moves the play along evenly. The drama is
carefully crafted, despite seeming deceptively simple.

Rich's first words parallel his political action throughout
the play and beyond, as we are told he eventually
becomes Lord Chancellor. Even his name suggests his
ambition. Cromwell's words to Norfolk, 'This isn't
Spain' (p. 61), echo Norfolk's words to Thomas More
uttered in the privacy of More's house. A wealth of
meaning is, then, attached to them, because Cromwell
must have had a verbatim report of what passed
between the two friends. The goblet More gives Rich
in a seemingly innocent scene returns later as a means
of attacking More. The 'Oh', Roper utters when he
hears Rich's name (p. 37) contains a condemnation of
Rich's character, though it is unspoken. It is all very
economically done.

The characters are extremely realistic: Henry's hurt
vanity when outshone by Margaret; Rich childishly
pestering Cromwell for promotion at the wrong time;

Roper's total commitment to opposing causes; Alice's failure to understand her husband; Rich claiming friendship with Norfolk and later hesitating to say, 'so help me, God' (p. 93), are all most convincing.

In spite of this, the main characters are also **symbols** (see Literary Terms). Thomas More represents individual conscience against powerful authority; Cromwell and Rich, naked political expediency and greed; Norfolk the ordinary decent aristocrat; Wolsey, a corrupt church; Cranmer, the church established by law, which will use the law against the old allegiances, and Henry, authority, driven by the need to maintain order in the kingdom. There are many in our day, at home and abroad, to whom these categories apply, which makes this a play for all seasons too.

The humour is muted and at times unspoken. There is gentle humour in More's second line when he asks Matthew if the wine is good, making it plain that he knows his steward helps himself to it. It is stronger when he answers, 'Ooh!' (p. 75) to the jailer's announcement that the secretary, the duke and the archbishop are waiting to interrogate him. It takes the form of **irony** (see Literary Terms) on occasion, as when Wolsey unselfconsciously tells More he should have been a cleric, meaning he was principled enough, and More answers, 'Like you, Your Grace?' (p. 13); or earlier in the same scene when Wolsey's remark, '… you could have been a statesman' receives the rejoinder, 'Oh, Your Grace flatters me' (p. 10). Wolsey is again unaware of the **irony** of his remark, whereas More clearly intends his words to mean the opposite of what they say.

Cromwell makes a number of **ironic** statements, from telling Rich that because the king has a conscience he wants More to agree to the marriage or be executed (his conscience is obviously selective), to using the word 'unhappily' when informing the court of the absence of Southwell and Palmer (p. 95). He remarks 'Brilliant' ironically (p. 77) when the Duke of Norfolk says they must find out what Thomas More objects to in the Act.

There is dramatic **irony** (see Literary Terms) in the boatman's words about Cromwell: 'The coming man they say, sir' (p. 14) and in More's estimation of himself that he is not 'the stuff of which martyrs are made' (p. 35). The vivid symbol (see Literary Terms) of the Thames silting up has already been mentioned.

Sarcasm (see Literary Terms) also plays its part. More uses it when he asks Cromwell whether the word 'conscience' is unfamiliar to him and again when he thanks Cromwell for letting him know that their conversation will be recorded.

The Common Man makes the play's first humorous statement when he says he would have shown us something of his own had he been allowed on stage naked. Humour arises from the foolishness of Rich, who begins writing down everything that is said before the interview between Cromwell and More begins. Thomas More tells Henry that the king's music sounds delightful to him, but that he has a deplorable taste in music and he pretends to threaten to bring Cromwell home to dinner.

The entire play has been called a metaphor (see Literary Terms). Be this as it may, it is certain that figurative language (see Literary Terms) abounds. The first speech in the play contains the image (see Literary Terms) of clothing, 'speaking costumes' (clothes denoting the owner's rank) and 'embroidered mouths' (high-flown speech); 'closely woven liturgical stuff' (complicated church worship), all of which are in direct contrast to the Common Man's dull appearance.

Sailing imagery (see Literary Terms) is in evidence as
More describes how he cannot navigate the 'currents
and eddies of right and wrong', which Roper finds
'plain-sailing' (p. 39). Indeed, the image of water is
prevalent throughout the play. The Thames becomes a
symbol (see Literary Terms) of the kingdom, which
looks 'very black' and is 'silting up' apart from a channel
in the middle that is 'getting deeper all the time'
(p. 16). More tells us that if Wolsey fell the 'splash'
would swamp the Mores' 'small boat' (p. 20). Henry
calls More's integrity 'water in the desert' (p. 32). At
the beginning of Act II, 'water under the bridge'
denotes the passage of time and what it has avoided are
'torrents' of religious zeal, which have been channelled
down the 'canals of moderation' (p. 47). More accuses
Roper of pulling in the anchor of his principles when
the weather gets rough and letting the anchor down in
calmer waters. He refuses to let Roper 'hoist her
[Margaret] up the main mast of his [Roper's] sea-going
principles' (p. 39).

The imagery More uses to describe the law is that of a
forest, wherein he can hide himself and his daughter,
for no-one knows the 'forest' of the law better than he.
Roper would 'cut down' every law so that in the end
there would be no protective 'forest' for anyone (p. 39).

# PART FOUR

# STUDY SKILLS

## HOW TO USE QUOTATIONS

One of the secrets of success in writing essays is the way you use quotations. There are five basic principles:
- Put inverted commas at the beginning and end of the quotation
- Write the quotation exactly as it appears in the original
- Do not use a quotation that repeats what you have just written
- Use the quotation so that it fits into your sentence
- Keep the quotation as short as possible

Quotations should be used to develop the line of thought in your essays.

Your comment should not duplicate what is in your quotation. For example:

**Wolsey wishes Thomas More would behave like a politician and says: 'If you could just see facts flat on, without that moral squint; with just a little common sense, you could have been a statesman.'**

Far more effective is to write:

**Wolsey is disappointed that Thomas More has moral scruples and feels that 'with a little common sense, [he] could have been a statesman'.**

However, the most sophisticated way of using the writer's words is to embed them into your sentence:

**Wolsey cannot understand Thomas More's 'moral squint' and admits that to be 'a statesman' he would need to abandon his principles.**

When you use quotations in this way, you are demonstrating the ability to use text as evidence to support your ideas - not simply including words from the original to prove you have read it.

Everyone writes differently. Work through the suggestions given here and adapt the advice to suit your own style and interests. This will improve your essay-writing skills and allow your personal voice to emerge.

The following points indicate in ascending order the skills of essay writing:

- Picking out one or two facts about the story and adding the odd detail
- Writing about the text by retelling the story
- Retelling the story and adding a quotation here and there
- Organising an answer which explains what is happening in the text and giving quotations to support what you write

..................................................................

- Writing in such a way as to show that you have thought about the intentions of the writer of the text and that you understand the techniques used
- Writing at some length, giving your viewpoint on the text and commenting by picking out details to support your views
- Looking at the text as a work of art, demonstrating clear critical judgement and explaining to the reader of your essay how the enjoyment of the text is assisted by literary devices, linguistic effects and psychological insights; showing how the text relates to the time when it was written

The dotted line above represents the division between lower and higher level grades. Higher-level performance begins when you start to consider your response as a reader of the text. The highest level is reached when you offer an enthusiastic personal response and show how this piece of literature is a product of its time.

Set aside an hour or so at the start of your work to plan what you have to do.

- List all the points you feel are needed to cover the task. Collect page references of information and quotations that will support what you have to say. A helpful tool is the highlighter pen: this saves painstaking copying and enables you to target precisely what you want to use.

- Focus on what you consider to be the main points of the essay. Try to sum up your argument in a single sentence, which could be the closing sentence of your essay. Depending on the essay title, it could be a statement about a character: From Thomas More's opening question about the quality of the wine, we understand his tolerance and gentle humour; an opinion about setting: The conversation between the boatman and Thomas More concerning the blackness of the night and the ever-deepening central channel in the Thames finds its echo in the dangerous and confused state of the country and the deepening crisis at its centre; or a judgement on a theme: When Thomas More declares that what is important is not whether he is right or wrong but that he believes he is right, he touches upon personal integrity, which lies at the very core of this drama.

- Make a short essay plan. Use the first paragraph to introduce the argument you wish to make. In the following paragraphs develop this argument with details, examples and other possible points of view. Sum up your argument in the last paragraph. Check you have answered the question.

- Write the essay, remembering all the time the central point you are making.

- On completion, go back over what you have written to eliminate careless errors and improve expression. Read it aloud to yourself, or, if you are feeling more confident, to a relative or friend.

If you can, try to type your essay, using a word processor. This will allow you to correct and improve your writing without spoiling its appearance.

*Examination essay*

The essay written in an examination often carries more marks than the coursework essay even though it is written under considerable time pressure.

In the revision period build up notes on various aspects of the text you are using. Fortunately, in acquiring this set of York Notes on *A Man for All Seasons*, you have made a prudent beginning! York Notes are set out to give you vital information and help you to construct your personal overview of the text.

Make notes with appropriate quotations about the key issues of the set text. Go into the examination knowing your text and having a clear set of opinions about it.

In most English Literature examinations you can take in copies of your set books. This in an enormous advantage although it may lull you into a false sense of security. Beware! There is simply not enough time in an examination to read the book from scratch.

*In the examination*

- Read the question paper carefully and remind yourself what you have to do.
- Look at the questions on your set texts to select the one that most interests you and mentally work out the points you wish to stress.
- Remind yourself of the time available and how you are going to use it.
- Briefly map out a short plan in note form that will keep your writing on track and illustrate the key argument you want to make.
- Then set about writing it.
- When you have finished, check through to eliminate errors.

*To summarise,*     • **Know the text**
*these are the*      • **Have a clear understanding of and opinions on the storyline,**
*keys to success:*      **characters, setting, themes and writer's concerns**
                    • **Select the right material**
                    • **Plan and write a clear response, continually bearing the question in mind**

## Sample essay plan

A typical essay question on *A Man for All Seasons* is followed by a sample essay plan in note form. This does not present the only answer to the question, merely one answer. Do not be afraid to include your own ideas and leave out some of the ones in this sample! Remember that quotations are essential to prove and illustrate the points you make.

**In your opinion, is *A Man for All Seasons* any more than a chronicle of events? Illustrate your answer by close reference to the text.**

Such a question anticipates a wide-ranging response and can be approached in a number of ways. An outline for your answer might look like this:

*Part 1*     It is certainly a chronicle of events.
   • The characters all existed.
   • The events actually happened.

In this part of the answer refer very briefly to the main characters and events.

*Part 2*     It is very much more than a chronicle: it is a morality play, too.
   • We have a representative of good in Thomas More: demonstrate from the text his humour, kindness, integrity, cleverness and courage.
   • There are representatives of evil: Cromwell – ruthless, officious, amoral, ambitious, ingratiating, sadistic;

Wolsey – impatient, ill-mannered, ambitious, ruthless, deceitful, amoral; Rich – weak, greedy, ambitious, corruptible. In this part of your answer you will need to make much more detailed reference to the text, showing where it illustrates the points you are making.

- The cause of the conflict is the king's dilemma. State very briefly the king's problem. Show how this reveals his character: vain, ruthless, emotional, determined.

*Part 3*   Each member of the audience is invited to consider the question of the importance of individual conscience in the lives of us all, if we are to operate as fully human beings.
- The conscience of the king.
- The conscience of Thomas More.
Is there a difference between them?

*Part 4*   Although, in many ways, the playwright uses the characters as symbols, the success of the play is largely due to the skill with which he makes the characters real and recognisable. Consider this in terms of: Norfolk, Alice, Roper, and the Common Man, demonstrating your points from the text.

*Part 5*   Conclusion: in this section, which should be quite short, sum up the earlier points in your answer. Far from being merely a chronicle, the play is a morality play, a challenge to the audience in their own lives and a fascinating entertainment.

This is not a definitive answer to the question and you may have other ideas, but the sample does indicate the way your mind should be working and the points to make in order to achieve a reasonably thorough essay.

Make a plan as shown above and attempt these questions:

1 What in your view are the contributions of: a) The Common Man and b) Thomas More's family to the success of the play? Support your answer from the text.

2 How realistic do you feel the characters are in this drama? Give evidence from the text for your opinion.

3 How successful is Robert Bolt in engaging our minds on the main themes? Verify your answer from the text.

4 Consider the importance and effect of the imagery employed in this play. What do you think it adds to the play as a whole?

5 Choose four characters, apart from Thomas More, with whom you sympathise. Discuss those aspects of their characters which enlist your sympathy.

6 In which way might this play be considered a metaphor for any age? Compare incidents in the play with their parallels in a different era.

7 In your opinion, is Thomas More rightly regarded as 'A man for all seasons'? Provide evidence from the play to support your answer.

8 Examine in detail the problems facing the king and Thomas More, as depicted in the play. Consider their personalities and sense of duty before giving your opinion as to whether or not More's stand was justified.

9 Select four characters who contributed in some way to Thomas More's execution. Discuss each one's contribution and motive, showing, in each case, whether there were any mitigating circumstances.

10 Demonstrate how Bolt manages to sustain the interest of the audience, despite the fact that the outcome of the play is known from the beginning.

# CULTURAL CONNECTIONS

## BROADER PERSPECTIVES

The themes of the play: power, and the abuse of power; corruption, both of the individual and the state; and moral integrity, are as relevant today as they were in the sixteenth century. You may be interested in reading other books involving oppressive regimes and their effect on the individual.

*The Crucible*, a play by Arthur Miller, was written during the notorious Senator McCarthy investigations against Communists in the USA in the early 1950s. Though it is ostensibly about the witch trials at Salem, Massachusetts, in 1692, it is really aimed at McCarthyism. John Proctor, who resists the injustice of the witchfinders, goes to his death knowing that the society in which he lives cannot differentiate between right and wrong.

There is a modern video of the play starring Daniel Day Lewis and Wynona Ryder.

*Murder in the Cathedral*, a play by T.S. Eliot, tells the story of the temptations and eventual murder of Thomas à Becket in an earlier struggle between the church and a king of England, in this case Henry II. This play has a Chorus, rather as *A Man for All Seasons* has the character of the Common Man. Becket, like More, is accused of acting from motives of vanity.

A not very good black-and-white film of the play was made in 1951.

*The Power and the Glory* by Graham Greene tells the story of an alcoholic priest operating clandestinely in Mexico where the church has been outlawed by a totalitarian government. Although the opposite of Thomas More as a person, the two characters have their integrity in common as the whisky-priest commits himself to his priestly duties before being caught and executed.

*1984* by George Orwell is set in a nightmare, totalitarian world from which freedom is absent. Winston Smith attempts to outwit the system but the full horror of the future is realised when the system defeats him by finding what his phobia is and using it to destroy him.

A colour film of the novel, starring John Hurt and Richard Burton, was made in 1984. It is much better than the black-and-white version made in 1955.

There is an excellent film of *A Man for All Seasons* for which Robert Bolt wrote the screenplay. It stars Paul Schofield, Wendy Hiller, Robert Shaw and Orson Welles among a fine cast. It is also on video.

Sadly, the effects of totalitarian regimes on the individuals caught up in them, whether as oppressors or victims, are not confined to plays and novels. Since the collapse of Communism and the end of the Cold War, there is an increasing number of books about life under this most oppressive of regimes. Most are written by its victims, trying to discover how and why their oppressors behaved as they did. *Stories* by the Russian writer Lev Razgon is a recent addition. Quietly and objectively the book describes his experiences and the people he met during two long periods of imprisonment in the huge prison camps in the Soviet Union. In a similar vein Primo Levi, an Italian Jew taken prisoner by the Nazis in the Second World War, described in his many books the atrocities committed by an equally brutal, though shorter-lived, regime. The lack of bitterness in his writing makes his indictment even more powerful.

And the problem is still with us. Think of any of the world's political trouble-spots and the chances are that there you will find corruption, oppression and the abuse of the law.

**blank verse** unrhymed lines of poetry, each line of which consists of five unstressed syllables where each unstressed syllable is followed by a stressed syllable

**chorus** usually a group of people who comment upon the action of the play

**colloquial** (language) the language of everyday use

**dramatic irony** the speaker of the lines does not understand their significance although the audience does. The term also applies when a character's words come back to haunt him or her later in the play

**figurative language** language which uses figures of speech

**figure of speech** imaginative use of language, generally in a non-literal fashion, for concentration of meaning or emotion or for ornament

**image/imagery** can be a literal picture, but is usually applied to language which uses simile, metaphor or other figures of speech

**ironic/irony** words that say the opposite of what the speaker means. A situation may also be ironic when a person's behaviour contradicts what he or she says about him or herself

**Machiavellian** someone who will do anything to achieve their ends, without a trace of morality

**metaphor** type of simile, in which something is spoken of as though it is something else, e.g. More refers to the law as a forest

**morality play** medieval play portraying the conflict between good and evil for the instruction of the faithful. Characters were representations of virtues and vices rather than realistic portayals of people

**Petrarchan sonnet** poem of fourteen lines, composed of a section of eight lines (octave) and six lines (sestet). The rhyme scheme is: abba abba in the octave and cde cde in the sestet

**prose** straightforward, unpoetic language

**rhyming couplets** two consecutive lines that rhyme

**sarcasm** sneering way of saying something

**simile** imaginative figure of speech comparing unlikely people or objects

**stanza** division of a poem consisting of a number of lines grouped together to form a pattern

**sub-plot** lesser action which carries on alongside the main action of the play

**symbol** person or object which represents something else

**theme** the main ideas present in the play, not the story itself

**transferred epithet** where the adjective is moved from the item it should apply to and attached to another, e.g. the Common Man mentioned speaking costumes

# TEST ANSWERS

**TEST YOURSELF (Act I Part 1 pp. 1–25)**

**A•••** 1 The Common Man *(p. 1)*
2 Richard Rich *(p. 2)*
3 Thomas More *(p. 4)*
4 William Roper *(p. 17)*
5 Henry VIII *(p. 11)*
6 Chapuys, the Spanish ambassador *(p. 21)*
7 Thomas More *(p. 22)*
8 Thomas More *(p. 23)*

**TEST YOURSELF (Act I Part 2 pp. 25–46)**

**A•••** 1 Thomas More *(p. 26)*
2 Henry VIII *(p. 29)*
3 Alice More *(p. 35)*
4 William Roper *(p. 36)*
5 Thomas Cromwell *(p. 43)*
6 Duke of Norfolk *(p. 28)*
7 Margaret More *(p. 28)*
8 Thomas More *(p. 46)*

**TEST YOURSELF (Act II Part 1 pp. 47–74)**

**A•••** 1 William Roper *(p. 48)*
2 Alice More *(p. 52)*
3 Thomas More *(p. 68)*
4 Thomas More *(p. 71)*
5 William Roper *(p. 48)*
6 Margaret More *(p. 55)*
7 Duke of Norfolk *(p. 60)*
8 Richard Rich *(p. 62)*

**TEST YOURSELF (Act II Part 2 pp. 74–99)**

**A•••** 1 Norfolk *(p. 76)*
2 Thomas More *(p. 79)*
3 Jailer *(p. 80)*
4 Margaret More *(p. 83)*
5 Alice More *(p. 85)*
6 Thomas Cromwell *(p. 93)*
7 Thomas Cromwell *(p. 79)*
8 Margaret More *(p. 84)*

# NOTES

# NOTES

# Notes

# NOTES

## GCSE and equivalent levels (£3.50 each)

Maya Angelou
*I Know Why the Caged Bird Sings*

Jane Austen
*Pride and Prejudice*

Alan Ayckbourn
*Absent Friends*

Elizabeth Barrett Browning
*Selected Poems*

Robert Bolt
*A Man for All Seasons*

Harold Brighouse
*Hobson's Choice*

Charlotte Brontë
*Jane Eyre*

Emily Brontë
*Wuthering Heights*

Shelagh Delaney
*A Taste of Honey*

Charles Dickens
*David Copperfield*

Charles Dickens
*Great Expectations*

Charles Dickens
*Hard Times*

Charles Dickens
*Oliver Twist*

Roddy Doyle
*Paddy Clarke Ha Ha Ha*

George Eliot
*Silas Marner*

George Eliot
*The Mill on the Floss*

William Golding
*Lord of the Flies*

Oliver Goldsmith
*She Stoops To Conquer*

Willis Hall
*The Long and the Short and the Tall*

Thomas Hardy
*Far from the Madding Crowd*

Thomas Hardy
*The Mayor of Casterbridge*

Thomas Hardy
*Tess of the d'Urbervilles*

Thomas Hardy
*The Withered Arm and other Wessex Tales*

L.P. Hartley
*The Go-Between*

Seamus Heaney
*Selected Poems*

Susan Hill
*I'm the King of the Castle*

Barry Hines
*A Kestrel for a Knave*

Louise Lawrence
*Children of the Dust*

Harper Lee
*To Kill a Mockingbird*

Laurie Lee
*Cider with Rosie*

Arthur Miller
*The Crucible*

Arthur Miller
*A View from the Bridge*

Robert O'Brien
*Z for Zachariah*

Frank O'Connor
*My Oedipus Complex and other stories*

George Orwell
*Animal Farm*

J.B. Priestley
*An Inspector Calls*

Willy Russell
*Educating Rita*

Willy Russell
*Our Day Out*

J.D. Salinger
*The Catcher in the Rye*

William Shakespeare
*Henry IV Part 1*

William Shakespeare
*Henry V*

William Shakespeare
*Julius Caesar*

William Shakespeare
*Macbeth*

William Shakespeare
*The Merchant of Venice*

William Shakespeare
*A Midsummer Night's Dream*

William Shakespeare
*Much Ado About Nothing*

William Shakespeare
*Romeo and Juliet*

William Shakespeare
*The Tempest*

William Shakespeare
*Twelfth Night*

George Bernard Shaw
*Pygmalion*

Mary Shelley
*Frankenstein*

R.C. Sherriff
*Journey's End*

Rukshana Smith
*Salt on the snow*

John Steinbeck
*Of Mice and Men*

Robert Louis Stevenson
*Dr Jekyll and Mr Hyde*

Jonathan Swift
*Gulliver's Travels*

Robert Swindells
*Daz 4 Zoe*

Mildred D. Taylor
*Roll of Thunder, Hear My Cry*

Mark Twain
*Huckleberry Finn*

James Watson
*Talking in Whispers*

William Wordsworth
*Selected Poems*

*A Choice of Poets*

*Mystery Stories of the Nineteenth Century including The Signalman*

*Nineteenth Century Short Stories*

*Poetry of the First World War*

*Six Women Poets*

## York Notes Advanced (£3.99 each)

Margaret Atwood
*The Handmaid's Tale*

Jane Austen
*Mansfield Park*

Jane Austen
*Persuasion*

Jane Austen
*Pride and Prejudice*

Alan Bennett
*Talking Heads*

William Blake
*Songs of Innocence and of Experience*

Charlotte Brontë
*Jane Eyre*

Emily Brontë
*Wuthering Heights*

Geoffrey Chaucer
*The Franklin's Tale*

Geoffrey Chaucer
*General Prologue to the Canterbury Tales*

Geoffrey Chaucer
*The Wife of Bath's Prologue and Tale*

Joseph Conrad
*Heart of Darkness*

Charles Dickens
*Great Expectations*

John Donne
*Selected Poems*

George Eliot
*The Mill on the Floss*

F. Scott Fitzgerald
*The Great Gatsby*

E.M. Forster
*A Passage to India*

Brian Friel
*Translations*

Thomas Hardy
*The Mayor of Casterbridge*

Thomas Hardy
*Tess of the d'Urbervilles*

Seamus Heaney
*Selected Poems from Opened Ground*

Nathaniel Hawthorne
*The Scarlet Letter*

James Joyce
*Dubliners*

John Keats
*Selected Poems*

Christopher Marlowe
*Doctor Faustus*

Arthur Miller
*Death of a Salesman*

Toni Morrison
*Beloved*

William Shakespeare
*Antony and Cleopatra*

William Shakespeare
*As You Like It*

William Shakespeare
*Hamlet*

William Shakespeare
*King Lear*

William Shakespeare
*Measure for Measure*

William Shakespeare
*The Merchant of Venice*

William Shakespeare
*Much Ado About Nothing*

William Shakespeare
*Othello*

William Shakespeare
*Romeo and Juliet*

William Shakespeare
*The Tempest*

William Shakespeare
*The Winter's Tale*

Mary Shelley
*Frankenstein*

Alice Walker
*The Color Purple*

Oscar Wilde
*The Importance of Being Earnest*

Tennessee Williams
*A Streetcar Named Desire*

John Webster
*The Duchess of Malfi*

W.B. Yeats
*Selected Poems*

Chinua Achebe
*Things Fall Apart*

Edward Albee
*Who's Afraid of Virginia Woolf?*

Margaret Atwood
*Cat's Eye*

Jane Austen
*Emma*

Jane Austen
*Northanger Abbey*

Jane Austen
*Sense and Sensibility*

Samuel Beckett
*Waiting for Godot*

Robert Browning
*Selected Poems*

Robert Burns
*Selected Poems*

Angela Carter
*Nights at the Circus*

Geoffrey Chaucer
*The Merchant's Tale*

Geoffrey Chaucer
*The Miller's Tale*

Geoffrey Chaucer
*The Nun's Priest's Tale*

Samuel Taylor Coleridge
*Selected Poems*

Daniel Defoe
*Moll Flanders*

Daniel Defoe
*Robinson Crusoe*

Charles Dickens
*Bleak House*

Charles Dickens
*Hard Times*

Emily Dickinson
*Selected Poems*

Carol Ann Duffy
*Selected Poems*

George Eliot
*Middlemarch*

T.S. Eliot
*The Waste Land*

T.S. Eliot
*Selected Poems*

Henry Fielding
*Joseph Andrews*

E.M. Forster
*Howards End*

John Fowles
*The French Lieutenant's Woman*

Robert Frost
*Selected Poems*

Elizabeth Gaskell
*North and South*

Stella Gibbons
*Cold Comfort Farm*

Graham Greene
*Brighton Rock*

Thomas Hardy
*Jude the Obscure*

Thomas Hardy
*Selected Poems*

Joseph Heller
*Catch-22*

Homer
*The Iliad*

Homer
*The Odyssey*

Gerard Manley Hopkins
*Selected Poems*

Aldous Huxley
*Brave New World*

Kazuo Ishiguro
*The Remains of the Day*

Ben Jonson
*The Alchemist*

Ben Jonson
*Volpone*

James Joyce
*A Portrait of the Artist as a Young Man*

Philip Larkin
*Selected Poems*

D.H. Lawrence
*The Rainbow*

D.H. Lawrence
*Selected Stories*

D.H. Lawrence
*Sons and Lovers*

D.H. Lawrence
*Women in Love*

John Milton
*Paradise Lost Bks I & II*

John Milton
*Paradise Lost Bks IV & IX*

Thomas More
*Utopia*

Sean O'Casey
*Juno and the Paycock*

George Orwell
*Nineteen Eighty-four*

John Osborne
*Look Back in Anger*

Wilfred Owen
*Selected Poems*

Sylvia Plath
*Selected Poems*

Alexander Pope
*Rape of the Lock and other poems*

Ruth Prawer Jhabvala
*Heat and Dust*

Jean Rhys
*Wide Sargasso Sea*

William Shakespeare
*As You Like It*

William Shakespeare
*Coriolanus*

William Shakespeare
*Henry IV Pt 1*

William Shakespeare
*Henry V*

William Shakespeare
*Julius Caesar*

William Shakespeare
*Macbeth*

William Shakespeare
*Measure for Measure*

William Shakespeare
*A Midsummer Night's Dream*

William Shakespeare
*Richard II*

William Shakespeare
*Richard III*

William Shakespeare
*Sonnets*

William Shakespeare
*The Taming of the Shrew*

William Shakespeare
*Twelfth Night*

William Shakespeare
*The Winter's Tale*

George Bernard Shaw
*Arms and the Man*

George Bernard Shaw
*Saint Joan*

Muriel Spark
*The Prime of Miss Jean Brodie*

John Steinbeck
*The Grapes of Wrath*

John Steinbeck
*The Pearl*

Tom Stoppard
*Arcadia*

Tom Stoppard
*Rosencrantz and Guildenstern are Dead*

Jonathan Swift
*Gulliver's Travels and The Modest Proposal*

Alfred, Lord Tennyson
*Selected Poems*

W.M. Thackeray
*Vanity Fair*

Virgil
*The Aeneid*

Edith Wharton
*The Age of Innocence*

Tennessee Williams
*Cat on a Hot Tin Roof*

Tennessee Williams
*The Glass Menagerie*

Virginia Woolf
*Mrs Dalloway*

Virginia Woolf
*To the Lighthouse*

William Wordsworth
*Selected Poems*

*Metaphysical Poets*

# York Notes – the Ultimate Literature Guides

York Notes are recognised as the best literature study guides.
If you have enjoyed using this book and have found it useful, you
can now order others directly from us – simply follow the ordering
instructions below.

## HOW TO ORDER

Decide which title(s) you require and then order in one of the following
ways:

**Booksellers**
All titles available from good bookstores.

**By post**
List the title(s) you require in the space provided overleaf,
select your method of payment, complete your name and
address details and return your completed order form and
payment to:

> *Addison Wesley Longman Ltd*
> *PO BOX 88*
> *Harlow*
> *Essex CM19 5SR*

**By phone**
Call our Customer Information Centre on 01279 623923 to
place your order, quoting mail number: HEYN1.

**By fax**
Complete the order form overleaf, ensuring you fill in your
name and address details and method of payment, and fax it
to us on 01279 414130.

**By e-mail**
E-mail your order to us on awlhe.orders@awl.co.uk listing
title(s) and quantity required and providing full name and
address details as requested overleaf. Please quote mail
number: HEYN1. Please do not send credit card details by
e-mail.

# York Notes Order Form

## Titles required:

| Quantity | Title/ISBN | Price |
|---|---|---|
| | | |
| | | |
| | | |
| | | |
| | | |
| | | |

Sub total _____

Please add £2.50 postage & packing _____

(*P & P is free for orders over £50*) _____

**Total** _____

Mail no: HEYN1

Your Name _____

Your Address _____

Postcode _____ Telephone _____

## Method of payment

☐ I enclose a cheque or a P/O for £_____ made payable to Addison Wesley Longman Ltd

☐ Please charge my Visa/Access/AMEX/Diners Club card
Number _____ Expiry Date _____
Signature _____ Date _____

*(please ensure that the address given above is the same as for your credit card)*

*Prices and other details are correct at time of going to press but may change without notice. All orders are subject to status.*

☐ *Please tick this box if you would like a complete listing of Longman Study Guides (suitable for GCSE and A-level students)*

🌑 York Press

📖 Longman

Addison
Wesley
Longman